Dedicated to my daughter, Katelynne Marie Jackson, and the memory of the lives and loves we've lost by wandering in sin. They are missed more each day. Also to Jim Taylor and the wonderful community of Bay Saint Louis, Mississippi.

THE SHADOW I CAST

BY

AJ JACKSON

TABLE OF CONTENTS

PREFACE BY THE AUTHOR

I know I alluded to the fact that I would not return to write more of my experiences, but things have changed in the last seven years. They have a way of doing that. My son, who just turned fourteen, seems to be growing in to a very well-adjusted and bright young man. My thirty-first birthday just passed, and I spent it here in this prison cell. Yes, if you did not know already, I have been incarcerated at a maximum security federal prison since 2006.

I still miss my Christi and hate the fact that I could not be there to watch my little Lenny grow up, but these are things that I cannot change. The best that I can do is hope that he reads my book and knows the circumstances regarding his return to Dexter were beyond his daddy's control and in his best interest.

I have done my time, quietly for the most part. I figure what better way to pass the time than writing.

This is not the first thing that I have written since my capture. I have written several poetry collections, and I plan to publish them upon my release. This is, however, the first time I have written about my life since writing *The Life and Times of America's Most Wanted*. It sold rather well I am told, so apparently people were intrigued to hear what I had to say about myself and my friends. The Red Cross raked in vast proceeds from its publication.

In this book I plan to pick up right where I left off, with Charlotte and me leaving Dexter. I will chronicle my days behind bars, journal style and include all pertinent correspondence. I want to bring you deep inside the prison where I have been detained. When my tale is told to completion, I want you to ask yourself if you feel justice has been served.

CHAPTER ONE:
RETURN TO THE OPEN ROAD

The miles I put between me and my son did nothing to ease the pain caused by our separation. The memory of his last words, spoken to me with tear-stained eyes, played over and over in my mind, "Daddy, I'm okay." Each time the burden became harder to bear. We were driving south through Arkansas when I finally had to pull over at a rest stop to collect myself.

Charlotte had gone inside to use the ladies room. In her absence, I walked alone into the shallow, manicured forest clutching the motel key from the Thrifty Oasis. A steady rain drizzled down in the darkness and fell cold on my skin. Street lamps illuminated the distance, far back on the concrete paths from which I had strayed. I longed for the silence, the stillness of a darkened sanctuary and found just that under an unremarkable tree.

With my head resting upon its uneven bark, I clenched my eyes tight, and in the darkness my past rushed upon me. I felt my soul flood over with sadness for all those I had loved and lost: Summer, Matt, Christi, my beloved, and Lenny. He was my legacy and my lone sense of redemption and security. All passed before my mind's eye leaving a longing for them in their wake I could no longer abide. Tears flowed freely, and my body quaked in my melancholy and shivered with coldness of that disconsolate night. The motel key, a relic of my last night with Christi, fell from my hand. I felt the warmth of a petite hand, soft and familiar return it to my hand and then slide across my shoulder.

It was Charlotte. I knew without her having to say a word. I welcomed her silence. I had no words for her. I had no words for anyone. I was a quaking, sobbing mass of emotion, and I needed only to let it all out without feeling compelled, out of convention, to convince others I was okay when I clearly was not. Still silent, she slid closer to me, and I turned into her embrace. My head came to rest on her shoulder. Her fingers ran reassuringly through my hair.

By the time I had collected myself we were both thoroughly rain soaked. Charlotte held me close as we trudged back through the rain and mud to the van, still warm and inviting. A security guard making his rounds drove slowly passed us but seemed to take no notice.

Charlotte opened the passenger door for me, kissed my forehead and closed the door. Minutes later we were once again southbound. "Get some rest, AJ. I'll wake you in a few hours."

I crawled into the back and stared at the ceiling, watching the lights of passing cars dance across it, until sleep finally overtook me.

When I woke up the van was stationary, and Charlotte was nowhere in sight. We were at a gas station, parked at the pump, and the sun was rising over whatever sleepy town we were in. A cop car was parked in front of the station. Inside I could see the officer pouring a cup of coffee and Charlotte walking right behind him coming from the restroom. She was calm, cool, and collected as always. She even stopped to mull over which breakfast sandwiches she wanted from the warmer, grabbed them and paid. The cop was behind her in line and never thought more about her than to check out her ass.

I realized then that, despite the short time we had known each other; I was going to miss this amazing young lady when I finally fulfilled my end of the bargain by getting her back to New Orleans. Traveling with her I had come to realize just how talented, adaptive, and kind-hearted she truly was.

I watched her make her way back to me, her stride confident and unaffected by the close proximity of the police. She noticed me awake, smiled, and held up the plastic sack. "Breakfast is served."

She took the passenger seat and watched me crawl across the cabin into the driver's seat. "Thanks. What'd ya get me?" I asked.

"Only the finest they serve in this Podunk town. Sausage biscuit wrapped tightly in plastic and heated for hours on end to perfection under heat lamps," she replied. I took the sandwich from her and just had to smile at her quick wit.

After only a bite I realized the taste would probably have been the same had I foregone removing the plastic wrap from the tasteless and tiny breakfast sandwich. "Where are we?" I asked, setting down my food and opening up the road atlas. Sure I could have opened up the laptop and searched online maps, but I had just gotten up and didn't have that kind of energy when a low-tech solution would suffice.

"Wynne, Arkansas."

I searched and searched but found it only when she leaned over, gazed and pointed me in the right direction. "I need to make a stop. It won't take long."

Her eyes met mine, and I knew that she was starting to feel the same attachment for me that I knew was growing in my heart. "I'm in no hurry."

I wanted to say something to make her realize that, although I had feelings for her also I would never act on them. I had only recently lost my Christi. I knew I would not be right for a long time, if ever. She deserved someone that could give her his whole heart, not just the shattered and battered bits I had left to offer. With all of this running through my head, my lips remained silent on the matter.

I let the police car leave the parking lot ahead of us. I wanted no surprises and wanted to afford him no chance to follow us out, run the tag and get suspicious. He left without incident.

As best as memory serves me we were about thirty miles west of Memphis at that time. The drive was short but still took us nearly an hour to get downtown for all the inbound morning traffic.

"AJ, why are we here, in Memphis? Isn't this

where…" she stopped.

"Yes, and in a minute you will see where it happened. I just need a few minutes when we get there."

"You sure you want to do this?" She asked.

"Yeah," I replied, obviously lying. I wasn't sure what I could handle at the time. I was fragile with my emotions raw, and the slightest injury or insult could be the salt to set me off. Something inside of me just had to return to the place my beloved friends had been taken from me.

The trashy little motel had not changed. It was exactly as I remembered it until I parked in front of what was once JP and Summer's room one night six long years ago. I could not believe my eyes as I gazed on a little plaque that had been screwed into the wall proudly proclaiming it as the room where Jeremy Phife was taken into custody. It made my blood absolutely boil with anger.

The murder of two of my dearest friends and the maiming and detainment of the third was not something that I appreciated the proprietor profiteering from.

This was not my brightest idea to be sure, coming back here to the scene of such a tragic massacre. My rage was fueled equally by the trespass and the lingering sadness of losing so many close friends. I realized then it was a wound that would never fully heal. Still, I needed relief right then, something to appease the darkness swelling within, and I knew exactly how to achieve it.

I said nothing to Charlotte as I backed up and drove away.

"AJ, you alright?" She asked.

"Yeah, just need to pick something up from the gas station, and we'll be on our way." She smiled, reassured that we would soon be leaving Memphis.

What I did not expound on was the plan brewing, like a hurricane over hot waters, in my brain. I felt like an almighty avenger who had come to set things right with a sword of blue hot flames, but my calm exterior masked a seething lake of fire in my soul that would soon flood its banks and rush out into the world.

I pulled into the first gas station that presented itself and told Charlotte to wait in the van. I swiped my cash card and filled an empty milk jug- that we usually kept refilled with water- with gasoline. Charlotte leaned out the window to comment.

"I don't know what you are planning, but you might as well top off the tank while you are at it." Despite my rage I could not help but appreciate the forethought she had, and I obeyed.

"You drive," I insisted as I climbed in on the passenger side. "I think you know where we are headed and remember how to get there."

We were back at the motel in a matter of moments. I got out with my makeshift gas can in hand. "Drive one block up to that fast food joint we just passed. Leave the motor running, and I will meet you in ten minutes. If I don't show up by then, head to New Orleans without me."

She was stone cold and in the moment. I could tell that she would not let her emotions get the best of her. If she needed to leave me behind, she would do as instructed without pause. Our eyes lingered upon each other for what we hoped would not be the last time.

I shut the door, made sure she was clear of the parking lot, and began my assault on the injustice that had caught my ire. The lot was empty, no people visible. Very little traffic filled the road beyond.

The door was before me, patiently awaiting my wrath. I opened the milk jug and dowsed the plaque with gas and set it ablaze. I raised an angry foot to the door, kicking it three hard times before it finally gave, swinging wide open.

I stepped inside, instantly remembering exactly where I had seen each of my fallen friends take their lasts breaths. I showered the walls and fixtures with gas. Every surface I encountered, I drenched: curtains, beds, mirrors, carpet. When the plastic jug was empty I discarded it haphazardly in the floor, lit the curtain, and walked out the door leaving the place to the cleansing flames.

Time was ticking away and I had a good amount of ground to cover before I would safely be back in my trusty van. Still, I could not run. It would draw too much attention should anyone notice the flames and smoke beginning to billow forth. Composure intact, I walked to the sidewalk and set a course for the meeting spot.

Apparently I had surpassed the given time before return because the van was fast approaching me. Charlotte pulled over and the door swung open. "Get in."

She looked down the road to the motel, now engulfed in flames. Her foot released from the petal and we were in motion before the door closed behind me. People were starting to gather as people always do in such times, but no notice was taken of us. If we were noticed as we fled it would be a long time before we would need to stop and refuel, chancing capture. The shadows had escaped the sunlight once again.

CHAPTER TWO:
MEMPHIS TO NEW ORLEANS

We drove due south, using I-55 to obtain some quick distance for about two hours before switching to the back roads I preferred. I kept Charlotte company in front while she drove. The persistent odor of gasoline permeated the van.

"I am sorry you had to witness that," I apologized, "but if you are going to try to make money off of someone's personal tragedy you have to understand that there will be repercussions." Charlotte's eyes never left the road. She merely nodded and sat silent for what seemed like an eternity.

At last she spoke, "I understand your reasons, AJ.

I do. You might have killed people today, innocent people." She looked in my direction, but I could not look her in the eyes. "If you don't find some way to release all this lingering anger you are never going to be able to wash all the blood from your hands."

"I know. Please don't think badly of me," I pleaded, ashamed that I let my emotions overrun me.

"AJ, I don't think you are a bad person at heart, but you are dangerous to yourself if not others." Her hand reached for mine, attempting to interlock her fingers between mine. I welcomed the warming contact.

"Perhaps, but soon enough you will be safely away from me. I would never do anything to hurt you, Charlotte."

"I should slap da hell out of you for even feeling like you had ta say that to me!" She smiled. "I see you, inside. Don't you get it, AJ?" She thought for a minute before continuing, "I been thinkin' about something. Maybe we could put off New Orleans for a bit longer? I wanna stay with you."

"Charlotte, we are going to New Orleans. I cannot give you what you need, what you deserve." I said.

"I deserve to be happy, I think, and I am happy with you," She countered content that her logic would win me over.

"Be that as it may, I am not what is best for you. You need a stable life and a stable man that you can lean on in rough times." I knew that she would again counter my argument, so I did not give her time to provide her rebuttal.

"Charlotte, I know these have been hard times

and we have leaned on each other to get through them. I know that you have feelings for me. I know I have feelings for you too, but I refuse to drag anyone else down. You see what this lifestyle has done to me, how it has hardened me. I don't want that for you."

Her eyes were still on the road, and a tear was sliding down her cheek. "Well, promise me that you will stay a few days in New Orleans. Don't leave me as soon as we get there. It is Carnival season. You can hide in the crowds. Just stay with me a few days, please?"

"I can do that for you. You know how much I love New Orleans anyways. Did you really think I was just going to put you out and take off without visiting my favorite city?"

We stopped just north of Jackson, Mississippi to refuel and change places. The sun was setting on another fucked up day in the life of America's most wanted as I walked among society without ever really belonging to it.

Charlotte, having the less famous face and a corresponding less chance of being recognized, pumped the gas and paid. I remained in the van adjusting the seat and making my driver's nest as I liked to call it.

She returned with a veritable feast of gas station junk food consisting of a few candy bars, bags of chips, colas, and two roast beef sandwiches she had nuked. She set mine beside me and climbed into the back with hers. I ate mine while driving as the night, my favorite time to drive, was upon me, and I saw no reason to waste those precious hours of darkness.

I turned up the radio for a little bit of classic rock music to soothe my soul while I commanded the big bastard of a van down a dark and winding back road in rural Mississippi.

The next four hours of the night were an uneventful blur of vast expanses of trees shrouded in darkness and the painted pavement's coming and going. It was a welcomed repetition that calmed me inside. Driving had always had that affect on me.

Come morning we would be overwhelmed with all the excitement we could handle. Yes, we would be arriving in New Orleans on Fat Tuesday, the biggest, wildest day of Carnival, and chaos was assured.

CHAPTER THREE:
FAT TUESDAY 2003 DAY

New Orleans was already bustling as we exited I-10 via the Vieux Carre exit. Canal Street was already alive with early birds staking claim to their territories along the Zulu parade route. Police were busy setting up their barricades. The people we passed ranged from the drunks spilling out of the quarter that had not slept yet to families setting up their lawn chairs and throw bags. Venders pushed cumbersome carts of over-sized and over-priced novelty beads and boas hoping to peddle their wares to the waiting masses.

I had been to New Orleans before, but as anyone that has attended Mardi Gras can tell you, coming during the festivities adds a whole new dimension to the city. You can be assured to seen a million things that you never thought you would see with your own eyes. Some things you see will excite you. Some things will haunt you. Never until you have the image burned into your brain will you be quite sure what you have just witnessed.

As we waited in the inbound traffic I witnessed a person wearing a black dress standing to piss on the wall at the intersection of Bourbon and Canal. I watched a balloon shaped like a penis break free from its owner and float through the fog and out of sight.

We inched nearer our destination, crawling in synch with the gridlock ahead of us. At every intersection police motorcycles were positioned, blue lights lit as their owners directed traffic and watched for trespasses. Sirens chirped all around. The high police presence made me uneasy, but the influx of hundreds of thousands of people seemed to be cloaking us quite nicely.

When we finally got checked into our hotel room and parked my second wind came. I was ready to enjoy the moment and damn the past and future. I wanted to drop into the anonymity and depravity and wear another made-up persona. Yes, I wanted to take on another road alias and be anyone except myself.

I changed shirts, sliding into my favorite blue and white checkered flannel, and asked, "You coming out with me?"

Charlotte rolled over on the bed. "I don't think so. I got some calls to make, and then I am gonna take a nap."

"Suit yourself," I said. "Be back in a bit."

I needed some cash. I had plenty of money but it was all on my card. I prefer cash, especially when I am drinking so I set out to find a mark to pickpocket. I made my way down Saint Charles to Canal and back up a block to my destination, Bourbon Street. The crowd was thicker on Bourbon and in the French Quarter in general. Bars were already open and the masses had clearly been taking advantage of them. Easy money was ripe for the picking.

Within a block I had already scored two hundred dollars. I made my way into one of the souvenir shops that dot Bourbon and acquired a masquerade mask to conceal my identity. The mask was gold and covered all of my face with the exception of my mouth, which would come in handy after my next stop.

Bourbon is comprised mainly of strip clubs, bars, restaurants, and souvenir shops. I was not in the mood to scope women yet, and I was not hungry. That narrowed things down a bit, so I stopped and bought me a self-proclaimed Huge Ass Beer to accompany me on my little people watching adventure.

Beer in hand and identity hidden, I felt ready to take from New Orleans the solace I sought so I continued through the reveling swells of boisterous people on Bourbon Street. I found myself smiling at the outlandishly costumed men and women I encountered. I saw walking curtains with the words "Free Mammograms" printed along the outside. I saw a woman with a foot thick, yard long fake cock thrown on her shoulder, and I wondered to myself if she considered herself the Queen of Penis Envy. A small, ragtag marching krewe tossed throws accompanied by jazz musicians. There were more Elvis's than I have ever seen anywhere; the legend still alive and well and thriving in the hearts of his fans.

As entertaining as the walking parades in the

French Quarter were proving to be, I wanted to catch one of the larger krewes in action. Specifically, the Zulu Social Aid and Pleasure Club which was due to roll soon. I inquired about the exact parade route for Zulu and was instructed to head back to the intersection of Bourbon and Canal. The crowd swelled and spilled back down Bourbon as I scouted out a place to watch the slowly approaching parade. The sounds of the approaching police escort and marching bands were audible though the procession had not yet made the turn from Saint Charles Avenue onto Canal. I sipped at my beer and listened in on conversations around me. Excitement was building as it approached, a sight long anticipated by the crowd. Some had been camped out all night, protecting their territory to ensure they had front a front row view and better chance of being bestowed with one of the Zulus' much sought after painted coconuts.

I know you are asking yourself right now, "Is it really worth all the time and effort just to watch a parade pass?" But the parades of Carnival in New Orleans are unlike any parade you have ever seen. Countless elaborately decorated floats roll by with sometimes twenty or more krewe members on each, tossing doubloons, stuffed animals, plastic toys, beads, and occasionally handing out a painted coconut.

At last in sight, the first marching band made the turn onto Canal banging their drums with all their might and filling the cold morning air with their jazz. Kids of all ages, part of dance programs, proudly representing their schools followed closely behind, dancing to the music of the nearest band to them.

Next to follow was a troop of muscular Nubian

men, shirtless and barefoot banging conga and dejambe drums. They wore feathered headdresses, white war-paint, and bushy white wool leggings.   As they proceeded past, the first float came into view.

Pulled forth by a large, powerful tractor and shaped by paper mache painted brightly with butterflies, rainbows, and blades of grass, it proved to be a spectacular sight; one I felt was clearly worth the wait. And it was only one of a multitude yet to come rolling by. A large billboard gave the float number and name, but I was too busy surveying the pageantry behind the sign to make note of its message. Throws were flying all over the place, sometimes by the dozens. What seemed like a million hands would reach for the sky every time floats neared them, begging for their trinkets. Sometimes they were rewarded, other times not. The mood and supply of the individual krewe member often the deciding factors in when and where they threw and to whom it would be bestowed upon.

I watched this for about a half hour, but after collecting my fair share of doubloons and beads, I decided to head back down Bourbon to buy another beer and take a piss. The two actions were delicately intertwined as most places required you make a purchase before using their facilities. Not so much to be rude as to keep control of their building.

By the time I reached Saint Peter Street I was ready for some relative quiet, though that itself is hard to find on Fat Tuesday. The crowd on Royal had thinned, compared only to Bourbon. I headed toward the river intent on relaxing in Jackson Square, just me and my half empty beer. Crossing Royal Street I could not help but stop and admire the antiques and paintings done by local artists in the display windows before moving on.

I ventured further down Saint Peter passing the building where Tennessee Williams wrote A Streetcar Named Desire, and soon I arrived at Jackson Square, greeted once again by loud, costumed crowds gathered outside of Saint Louis Cathedral. Cameras snapping off photos and camcorders panning all around me made me glad that I was masked. The feel outside the square was different than back on Bourbon though. Here it was obvious that many of these people knew each other, like extended families having their annual reunion during a time of carefree communion. It was nice, watching them exchange their throws, bought in bulk months ahead of time to share with their friends.

I weaved through the crowds, finally taking a few minutes to rest and finish my beer on Decatur Street. I joined the many tourists lounging on some steps overlooking the street performers. Marionettes dangled and danced from strings being pulled from above while lip synching a James Brown song. Out of habit I scanned my surroundings in regular intervals, never letting myself get tunnel vision. In front of me sat a couple wearing matching Just Married caps. Propped by their feet rested a portrait of the newlyweds done in chalk. The detail of the drawing was surprising.

I thought of the family portrait that Charlotte had created at Ben's house and how perfectly she had captured Christi's likeness. The longing for Christi returned, heavy on my soul, like a weight Atlas could not hold up. I downed the rest of my beer and left the cup on the stairs. I needed my Christi, but I would have to settle for another beer.

Across the street, by the wrought iron fencing of Jackson Square proper, I found the progenitor of the portrait. Other examples of his skill decorated his work space and advertised his abilities. He had talent no question, but he was no Charlotte Savoy.

Tarot readers lined the left and right side of the square with a spattering of artists selling their canvases mixed in for good balance. Living statues- people spray painted gold or silver- struck and held poses for eternities freaking out the unsuspecting tourists as they passed, eliciting tips for their jars.

Near Café du Monde I turned toward the mighty Mississippi and the Moonwalk that overlooked her muddy waters. The Canal Street Ferry was en route to Algiers, silently transversing the watery expanse. All the sounds of the city's celebration- jazz musicians, sirens and horns, shouts, and random bits of conversations- stayed with me muffled in the distance as I found an empty bench and continued to sip my second Huge Ass Beer of the morning.

The motion of the water's surface lulled my mind back to thoughts of Christi. She should be here now with me with little Lenny between us on this cold bench. My child should have been attending with me earlier to catch a multitude of throws.

I know you are all wondering just how I would even consider taking my child to Mardi Gras, but that just shows your ignorance of the true nature of the celebration. Mardi Gras varies from one side of Canal Street to the other. If you are in the French Quarter, yes, expect the Girls Gone Wild version of it, complete with cross-dressers, drugs, booze, beads, and boobs. However, if you are on the CBD- Central Business

District- side of Canal, particularly along Saint Charles Avenue, you get an entirely different Mardi Gras experience. It is one that is more in tune with the Mardi Gras of old, remains sanitized for the most part, and is family friendly. When I refer to wishing my child and companion were there with me to experience this wonderfully old and culturally rich city, this is the side to which I would have had them exposed.

"You gonna finish that beer, man?"

I looked down into my oversized go-cup at the nearly gone beer quickly warming beyond my preferential temperature for drinking. The girl asking for it had to be homeless and looked a hot damn mess. I handed it to her. "Knock yourself out. I was planning on replacing it with a cold one here in a few anyways. What's your name?"

"Amy."

She was once very attractive and very well could still be if she cleaned herself up. Her red hair was a mess of tangles. She looked far too young to be wandering the street alone- let alone legally drink the beer I had just given her. But since when did I give a damn about breaking the law? She stood before me alternately drinking the beer and dragging a dying cigarette. I guessed she was a natural red-head due to her very pale complexion. She had piercings in her ears and one in her nose. Her shirt was a red and black checkered flannel buttoned only by the bottom two buttons, revealing a punk rock tee shirt below. Her cut off blue jean shorts surely were once full length pants as they were very short and rolled up at the bottom. A small pocket knife's outline instantly stood out to me- as did her shapely ass-, having worn a hole in said pocket, telling me that this was probably one of very few changes of clothes she owned. Black stockings ripped to shit over one knee and all over on the other leg covered most of her lower extremities.

"Those are my friends over there," she pointed to her two male companions yards away near a different bench. "That's Que. The drunk bastard is Danjo, ignore him." I looked them over and wondered what had brought them to this point in their young lives.

The one she called Danjo looked to be roughly the same age as Amy. He was wearing a black band shirt with black overalls unfastened from the top. His long nasty black hair crowned with what looked to be a train conductor's hat. Tattoos covered most of his exposed flesh, including sections of his lips. He too was pierced in various locales. The reason he had not walked up to me when she had was clear. First, as any bum knows a woman has a much higher sympathy rating and tends to be perceived as less of a threat when panhandling. Second, he was completely and totally shitfaced already. The expression piss drunk was brought into existence to perfectly describe the state this young vagrant found himself in. He had literally pissed himself, and I had no interest in getting closer to try to decipher his slurred speech or accept his handshake.

I have never been one to look down on others without cause, but there are some people you just don't feel like making life-long friends with, and Danjo- and Que for that matter- was a person of that certain disposition. Danjo- I noticed over Amy's shoulder as we talked- had found his feet briefly in an attempt I assume to walk over to us, but he staggered back and the bench took his legs out from under him, delivering him to the waiting concrete.

"Your friend," I interrupted, "just busted his head open. Might wanna check on him." Amy didn't even bother to turn and look.

"He's already on my fuckin' shit list today." She turned, finally in his direction and compassionately continued, "Lucky I haven't fuckin' rolled his stupid ass in the goddamn river already!" And with that went right back to what she had been previously talking about.

She told me she was from Massachusetts originally, but she had run away from home a few years ago. When she tired of telling me her story, which was well rehearsed to evoke the maximum amount of emotion in the listener, she started asking questions about me and where I was from. I just didn't feel like exerting the effort to make up any back story at the time so I politely excused myself and headed for the nearest cold beer I could buy.

Beer in hand, I wondered aimlessly around the French Quarter picking pockets and drinking before finally returning to the hotel room and Charlotte. I swiped my key card in the door and entered to find our room warm, the bathroom mirrors still steamy from Charlotte having showered before laying down for her morning nap.

The alcohol had taken effect in me probably two beers and three shots of jagermeister back, and I found myself the drunkest I had been in some time. I was mellow and reflective, but still managed to give my sadness the slip and not become depressive. I took off my beads and jacket and leaned against the wall, watching Charlotte sleep.

She was cuddled up snug under the blankets- that probably had not been cleaned in God knows how long- with them pulled up to her chin. The noise of the festivities outside intruded ever so often even though we were on the twelfth floor facing away from the French Quarter. Something inside me desired to kiss her despite everything. Still, I resisted the urge. The alcohol was bringing feelings to the surface best kept from it.

I decided that Charlotte had the right idea, and that a nice hot shower and nap were in order. Tonight promised to be one to remember, and there was no sense spoiling it by being too exhausted to enjoy it properly.

I staggered into the bathroom and began disrobing, not bothering to shut the door, let alone lock it. I twisted the knobs and felt to make sure the water's temperature was to my liking before stepping inside.

The water pressure sucked, as it always seemed to in New Orleans, but I did not particularly care. The steam began to build filling the shower, the room, and eventually spilling out into the rest of the hotel room. After cleaning up I could not bring myself to leave the comfort of the scalding hot water right away, so I simply leaned against the wall and let the water continue to rain down on me hot. That shower, like all simple pleasures in life, eventually must be brought to an end.

With a few flicks of my wrist to turn off the water and slow steady step out onto the tile, it was done. I grabbed a towel and dried my hair and face. I could see the floor and another, fairer pair of legs accompanying my own from below the towel. Pulling it from my face

I found Charlotte standing before me, watching me as I stood naked before her.

Her lips were slightly parted, full and inviting. I lowered the towel and wrapped it around my waist. She walked to me, stopping inches away, so we were face to face, and said, "Come lie down and get some rest." Before I knew it, her lips were on mine, and I was kissing her back. It was not full of passion, simply soft and inviting, and I answered with a simple nod and without words.

She followed me, still naked except for my damp towel, to the bed and slid under the covers after me. "Your towel is all wet," she said, sounding still half asleep, and tugged it away and dropped it into the floor. She cuddled up to me, her arm across my bare chest, far from dry. I lay there for some time staring at the ceiling before sleep came.

CHAPTER FOUR:
FAT TUESDAY 2003 NIGHT

The noise of sirens below brought me back to the waking world. Charlotte was still cuddled up to me in a most intimate manner, fully clothed. I glanced to the alarm clock on the night stand beside the bed. It was nearly six in the evening.

Charlotte stirred. She stretched, rubbed her eyes, and looked to me. "What do you think of Mardi Gras so far?" she asked.

"It is definitely an experience I won't be forgetting any time soon," I said, "but that is as much due to you as to everything outside." The embrace we still maintained had a warm, safe and secure quality to it. It was like nothing could harm us, if only we stayed cuddled up in that bed for all eternity; a modern day John and Yoko.

Truth be told, I would have been perfectly fine

with that. I missed holding another close and feeling the warmth. I missed human contact and realized only now just how rarely I touched anyone or was touched by others.

I told Charlotte about my wanderings while she had been resting. I spoke of the vagabonds I had met on the Moonwalk, of how different Bourbon Street was during Mardi Gras, and finally of how magnificent I had found the Zulu parade to be. All the while my fingers ran through her hair.

"Well, get up and get dressed. There's a' plenty left to see," she said. She leaned in and kissed me. Still, I did not move. As I said, I had finally once again found a Golden Moment I cared not to release, at least not yet.

Playfulness had overtaken her; now she was well-rested and rambunctious. She eased over on top of me, straddling me in all my nakedness and held each of my hands down. She grinded against me, and my body responded instantly. "Dat's more like it. So you did hear me tell you to get up." Her smile had grown mischievous. Her eyes sparkled deviously, and she released her hold on my wrists. Her nails slid down my arms, my chest, until finally she had a hold of me.

A sigh escaped her lips as her hand caressed and pulled me. She leaned closer to me and whispered, "While we are out tonight, keep dis' thing put away. Don't need any riots starting." She released her grip and crawled off of me and the bed. She picked the discarded towel up off the floor and laid it on the dresser.

I continued to lay there, amazed by her sudden boldness. She pulled off her pajama bottoms and shirt, revealing her bare breasts and black panties. She shimmied into her strapless black top and red and black school girl skirt as I called it. She was truly a sight to behold. She excused herself to the bathroom for a moment and then returned.

I watched her brush her long silky hair and tried to figure her out. Was she trying to seduce me into staying with her? Was she just teasing me? In the mirror she met my gaze.

"Don't make me come back over there. Get up." She was still toying with me. She knew that I had to get up naked and retrieve my clothes. If she wanted another peek that badly, so be it. I threw my legs over the side of the bed and stood up, walked passed her still aroused. Her eyes followed me as I made my way to the bathroom to retrieve my clothes.

I dressed and returned to find her still silently smiling to herself. I approached her, still primping in the mirror, grabbed her arm and whirled her around to face me.

"You gonna be like this all night?" I inquired.

"Probably," was her reply.

We smiled and kissed once again before heading out of the Central Business District on our way to the French Quarter. We had to skirt the parade route and come back down the opposite side of Canal to get to Bourbon Street.

We were going to grab a bite to eat at Krystal's, but the lines were long. We opted instead to get a Lucky Dog from one of the many street vendors posted up at each block, ready to service the masses in search of sober-up food. For those that do not know, a Lucky Dog is a chili dog on steroids basically, and they are fantastic. No Mardi Gras is complete without at least one Lucky Dog.

The crowds were unlike anything I had ever seen before. Bourbon Street was literally a sea of people, swaying and sloshing about like beer in a Huge Ass Beer go-cup. To move you had to be keen at detecting the current and riding it as far as it would take you. Wherever some young co-ed was willing to bare her breasts for meaningless beads you saw a swell in density, and I admit I was quick to join their ranks to catch a peek, illuminated by countless camera flashes capturing the moment for posterity and internet infamy.

Charlotte was solicited many times to flash her breasts, but she always declined. Part of me was saddened by this, wanting to look upon her supple breasts, but I knew that if I wanted, the view and more would be mine when we returned to our hotel room for the night. Still something about having her bare them for the admiration of total strangers really turned me on.

More than once I had to intervene as guys beyond wasted attempted to grab on her. They always backed off quickly and more often than not, I left the encounter with a freshly procured wallet. Mardi Gras, I was thinking, should become a regularly attended event for me, for the money making potential if nothing else.

About ten we staggered into the Cat's Meow, which was awesome, I might add. What is not to love about a karaoke bar where strangers from around the world gather to get wasted and sing shitty songs live over the internet? A window behind the performance stage, open onto Bourbon Street, let the passing crowd view the blackmail fodder free from the street. Not that anyone is really guarding the door that closely, after all

Charlotte was under twenty-one and was admitted and served without question.

The bar was packed, people bumping into each other, like atoms colliding continuously. No one seemed to care though. Polite excusals followed every unintended interaction. The same short list of songs got recycled over and over, allowing for no variety of songs sang, but the people wandering in and out of the doors opening onto Bourbon didn't seem to notice.

I grabbed one of the song lists and scanned it. Never before had I had the urge to get up in front of people and sing, but something possessed me to do so on this particular night. After all, it was Fat Tuesday. It was the Farewell to the Flesh. It was Mardi Gras, and if that is not the time to cut loose, when is?

I smiled that smile that meant that I was in the mood to get into some trouble Charlotte's way, and said, "I'll be right back." She looked at me, concern written across her face.

I accosted the host, stating that I wanted to sing a little ditty called "Jack and Diane", and she added my name- Davy- to the blackboard of upcoming performers.

I made sure to finish the rest of my beer and have a fresh one ready to take on stage with me. People were smoking all around the bar, and the peculiar smell of one cigarette smelled unlike any I had ever smelled before. I searched out the source and inquired what they were smoking and what it was called. It was a clove cigarette, a black. The guy offered me one and I instantly lit it up.

It tasted like candy heaven. The smoke billowing from the clove was so sweet of scent and taste that I could not get enough of it, even though I never really liked smoking cigarettes. Charlotte said it smelled good and took a drag.

I don't know if it was because I was not a big smoker or just that cloves smoke longer than regular cigarettes, but I was barely halfway done with it when my name was called to sing. I handed the rest to Charlotte and me and my beer made our way to the stage.

A beer in one hand, a mic in the other, I prepared myself to serenade this sea of strangers. I found Charlotte, watching in the crowd, still dragging on the clove and smiling up at me. I made sure my mask was still doing its job since I was being broadcast over the internet webcam, and I raised the mic to my mouth.

A million times I had sung this song driving down the road, but it is quite different when your voice is amplified and up for the world to scrutinize. I struggled at first, but soon I was belting out the lyrics like I wrote them myself.

The crowd sang along and clapped and hollered. I felt like a rock star, and wanted nothing more than to pull my mask from my face, tempt fate with one grand chance to capture me in all my blazing karaoke glory. The notion I luckily chalked up to the alcohol's influence and resisted.

Leaving the stage, I found myself swarmed by people wanting to shake my hand or kiss me or tell me how awesome I performed. In the jolt and jostle, my mask fell to the floor and would have been stomped to bits if Charlotte had not gathered it up for me. I kept my head down, away from the ever-watchful eye of the webcam until Charlotte had slide the mask back over my infamous face.

It was nearing midnight, the end of the orgy of indiscretions, as we staggered out of the Cat's Meow and headed back to our hotel room in the Central Business District. Three blocks from Canal, we heard the clock call the witching hour followed by police bullhorns. Mounted police lined up across the street trotted in unison driving the crowds out of the French Quarter. The crowd thickened as people were pushed closer together being pushed out of Bourbon Street. At times there was barely room to breathe. Charlotte held my hand tightly so we would not get separated in the mayhem. I once again took advantage of the situation and managed to snag a few more wallets, much emptier than the ones earlier in the day though, drained surely by alcohol, beads, and tips for titties.

Imagine a mosh pit of drunks several blocks long with pressure being applied steadily to one side, and that will give you a pretty clear picture of our surroundings. The BUB, which stands for Beer, Urine, and Barf, and discarded go-cups, and broken beads made it quite easy to lose your footing. Several fights broke out as people unintentionally staggered or fell upon one another. We were glad to be out of the thick of it when we finally made it to the intersection of Bourbon Street and Canal Street.

It was there that we met a very colorful character, the self-proclaimed Mayor of Bourbon Street. He was a black man wearing a top hat and tuxedo, complete with tails. We did not talk long with this fellow, as we had seen about all we cared to for the night, but he did impart one bit of wisdom that has remained with me to this day before we returned to our room. He told

Charlotte, "Hold your man close, darlin' cause New Orleans is a town of one-way streets, two-way women, and three-way guys."

Charlotte and I chuckled to ourselves. Our eyes caught for second, and I replied, "She doesn't have to worry. She not getting rid of me that easily." I pulled her close, and we walked down a ravaged Canal Street like two people in love.

"What was that about? Back there?" She inquired.

"I don't know. Maybe tonight has made me realize that I am not ready to let you go." We stopped, waiting for the traffic to clear so we could cross the street. "That is, if you still want to stay with me?"

She smiled but said nothing.

The elevator was full, and we didn't feel like waiting for the next one so I led Charlotte to the stairs. We were several flights up, and as Charlotte walked ahead of me I could not take my eyes off of her long legs and slowly swaying hips.

She turned, glancing back down at me over her shoulder and smiled. I missed a step and without thinking reached for her to right myself. Instead, I only managed to have us both collapse, me on top of her, on the stairs.

Neither of us was hurt. In fact, we again descended into a short bout of laughter. "If you want me that bad, you just gotta ask," Charlotte hissed.

"I do want you that bad," I replied.

"Well?" She said.

"Well, what?" My mind was not keeping up splendidly after so much booze.

"Well, ask already!" She commanded.

Her playful and dominating manner ignited in me a passion I could not ignore. "I'm asking."
She removed the masquerade mask from my face and kissed me furiously, letting her nails dig ever so slightly into the nape of my neck. Interrupting the kiss, she said, "About fucking time, AJ!"

Still sprawled out on the stairs, Charlotte below me, I turned to face her completely. Her legs widened, inviting me closer. My lips brought kisses that trailed down her neck to the top of her breasts, heaving with excitement. My hands at her sides, I tightened my grasp and brought the top down enough to expose her breasts to the pleasures of my wanton lips and tongue. Her fingers glided through my blond hair as she held me close to her bosom.

This was madness, giving in to such careless lust in a public stairwell, but neither of us cared. We were in the moment, swimming in a sea of passion that both of us would rather drown in than swim safely to shore.
I reached under her skirt and discovered the reason she had left the room after dressing earlier. She had been taking off her panties, for my fingers felt none, just smoothly shaven skin longing for my touch. Her body quivered upon my finger's first entry, and her arm reached for mine. Just as I was assuming that she was biding me stop, she pushed my fingers deeper and kissed me with rekindled abandon.

Soon her hand was working at the zipper on my blue jeans, but before she could grab a hold of me, we heard people approaching from a few flights of stairs below us. We got to our feet and righted our disheveled attire before they reached us, and we decided that this was a party best concluded in the privacy of our room.

A couple was arguing down the hall from us. I dug through my pockets for my key card to get us into the room. The guy, a big burly fucker, was pissed because his girlfriend had kissed some guy apparently. He slammed a vase into the carpeted floor, a mess of water and roses and broken glass resulting.

His woman was crying and trying to back away from him. He reared his fist back and punched one of several mirrors lining the hallway. I swiped my key card and Charlotte remained in the hall. My suitcase was open as fast as I could get to it, retrieving a little .22 caliber I always kept under my pillow. I pulled Charlotte into the room and stepped into the middle of this cluster-fuck waiting to happen.

The mountain of a man had his hand at the woman's neck, choking the life out of her. I eased up behind the guy and let the barrel of the gun dig hard into the back of his neck. He froze but did not release his death grip until I commanded him to let her go.

The woman dropped to the floor, holding her neck and sobbing. She crawled away from the brute and her defender, towards the door to our room, which was still open. Charlotte came to her aid.

The shattered mirror reflected hundreds of images of my face back at the subdued attacker. "I know you," he uttered.

"If that is true, then you know what I am capable of doing to you, and you better believe that I won't hesitate to end you right here and now!" I looked at Charlotte and nodded, and she left the woman's side.

She knew as well as I did, that our plans had just changed. We were leaving New Orleans a bit early. We had packed light, so she had all of our belongings packed up in no time, and was in the process of wiping everything down for fingerprints when I returned.

"What did you do to them?" She asked.

"Not that. I pistol whipped the bastard and knocked him out. Not sure how long he's gonna stay that way. The woman I simply told to stay put for two hours. I cut the phone cord so hopefully that will buy us enough time to get outta town."

The drive out of New Orleans was nothing short of the chaos we had experienced walking in the French Quarter. Not all of those people were leaving town, but a good majority of them were traveling out. It took us forever to get a comfortable distance away with all the wrecks. It is to be expected when you have that many drunks on the road and only a handful of long ass bridges as exits from the city.

It was a disappointing end to a night that had held so much promise. It was the reoccurring theme that I call my life.

CHAPTER FIVE:
STARTING OVER

For once in my life I didn't feel like I was really running away, but rather towards something. Of course we were always running away from our past, such is the nature of being "on the run", but Charlotte and I were running toward a new life, together. I knew, in all likelihood, I would end up full of regret for getting involved with another so soon after Christi, but I also knew that Christi would have wanted me happy. Living life the way we had for so long had shown us time and time again just how little guarantees life gives you. If you find someone that you can love and loves you equally, you better take it, because you are not promised the luxury of a tomorrow in which you can search for love.

Despite a constellation of mistakes that I had made over the years, I knew I had lived a charmed life in my own way. I had known the love of a wonderful woman, had been given the blessing of an amazing son, and had enjoyed the companionship of great friends. Sure I had also lost all of those things, but at least I had them to lose.

For whatever reason we were running, we did not run far. Less than a hundred miles from New Orleans, we stopped for gas in the small Mississippi community of Bay Saint Louis.

I pulled a twenty dollar bill from my pocket and had Charlotte pay for the gas. She returned with a few cokes and a large sandwich for us to share. I pumped the gas, and let her take over the driving.

"Just drive around the side streets for a few. I wanna check out how much we made in New Orleans off the wallets," I said.

I had accumulated fourteen wallets in one day. The cash totaled up to nearly three thousand dollars! Never mind all the credit cards because I rarely had the nerve to try and use them. Other things I found of value: thirty dollars worth of gift cards to Wal-Mart and eighty dollars worth of gift cards to various restaurants. It was a nice take.

I tried to hand Charlotte a few hundred dollars to keep on her, but she told me to hang on to it because she didn't have any pockets in her skirt. Somehow or another we ended up over on a road called Beach Boulevard, obviously because it faced the bay.

"Pull over in that parking lot on the left," I

instructed. Little more than the smell and sounds of the sea gave away the fact that a large body of water loomed in the darkness. The parking lot belonged to the school called Saint Stanislaus- a catholic school- across the street.

"I want to walk on the beach," Charlotte said. "Want to join me?"

It was chillier in Bay Saint Louis, which lacked New Orleans' tall buildings to obstruct the wind, but if Charlotte wanted to walk the beach I would be right there by her side.

We grabbed our jackets and locked up the van. The beach was literally right across the sandy street. We walked hand in hand and talked.

"I knew you would not let that stand back at the hotel." Charlotte commended me. "I knew you could not turn your back on that woman." I said nothing. I couldn't tell her that it took all of my strength to resist looking the other way. It took all my courage to confront that beast of a man. She continued, "I have cared about you for awhile now, but that was when I knew that I…"

I stopped her. I did not want to hear that word just yet. It was too early for that. Sure we were embarking on a new relationship together, but I could not yet listen to that word that I had for so long held synonymous with Christi.

How did I stop her? Well, I pulled her to me and kissed her. I didn't want things to be awkward, and to be honest I still wanted her tonight. Her scent had filled the van and kept lustful thoughts in the back of my mind all the way out of New Orleans.

The kiss tasted cosmic for lack of a better term.

Each times our lips met, they learned better their counterparts. She was becoming home to me, like I never thought another woman could. It scared the hell out of me, the big bad alleged criminal mastermind.

I broke the kiss at last, but the tender embrace we held. In that moment, I found clarity and knew what I wanted more than anything that was a possibility of actually obtaining, and I vocalized it, "What would you say if I said that we should get a hotel room, and in the morning maybe look for a place to rent here in Bay Saint Louis?"

She looked up into my eyes. Her baby brown eyes were glistening in the moonlight. "Wow, you want to actually live together, in a structure without wheels?"

"I didn't say that," I joked. "I am sure we can find a nice trailer park nearby." To make sure my humor was understood I pointed to the mansions further down Beach Boulevard. She hugged me tighter.

We drove around for a few minutes in search of a hotel, which we finally did find. I waited in the van and devised my plan while Charlotte got us a room for two days.

While I waited for Charlotte, I worked out the details in my mind. What could we afford and for how long? How would I be able to support us after our funds depleted? How could I keep from being recognized in such a small town as Bay Saint Louis?

I looked through the driver's licenses that had come from the stolen wallets. I studied each one until I found what I was looking for. Preston Myers. He was the same height and weight as me. Same overall bone structure and eye color. He wore his black hair shorter and had a beard. I could work with this.

Charlotte hopped back into the van and tossed me a key card. We didn't bother bringing in more than one suitcase each. It was nearly four in the morning by this point, and we would not be up long.

Our room was nothing fancy, but neither of us cared. We just wanted a big bed that we could stretch out across. The heat was a nice addition, but it was non-essential. After all, we could generate our own heat if we got too cold.

We sat our suitcases on the bed, unzipped them, and picked out the items that met our few immediate needs; toothbrushes, toothpaste, sleeping attire, and of course my pistol for under the pillow.

"Tomorrow, I need you to run to Wal-Mart for me. I need some hair dye, I going black with it. Gonna need your help with that and a haircut." I held up Preston's identification, and Charlotte agreed it should be close enough resemblance to pass.

She unfastened her skirt and let it fall to the floor. Her top followed soon after, leaving her standing naked and perfect before me. "I am going to shower real fast. Be right back." She threw her arms around me, kissed me one last time, and headed for the bathroom.

I collapsed on the bed, still clothed, clutching a pair of clean boxers I would sleep in after my shower. My eyes closed and a shallow sleep found me. No dreams came to haunt or taunt or tease, and before I was ready for my turn Charlotte cracked open the bathroom door.

Steam rolled out into the room, from which she emerged with a tiny white towel tightly enveloping her, pushing her breasts high and creating deep cleavage. She went about blow-drying her hair. The noise was enough motivation to finally get me in the shower.

No lingering under the hot water this morning, I was ready to get between the sheets and rest my weary bones. When I returned, Charlotte had already turned out the lights and crawled under the covers. Her eyes were closed.

The night ended with a bang-less whimper, but that was fine by me. We were embarking on a new life together, and there would be plenty of time to get to know the heart, mind, soul, and body of this phenomenal creature the gods named Charlotte Savoy.

We cuddled close and simply slept. It was nearly noon when we finally crawled out of bed. I returned my pistol to the suitcase so house-keeping would not discover it. There were many things we needed to accomplish today. The new hairstyle was only a part of it. We needed to scout for places to rent, and I needed to find a job.

That is how serious I was about this plan. I was ready to settle into the lifestyle of a square, if it meant safety and security for Charlotte. I thought of my son, and how great it would have been to have him with us. As great of an idea as it seemed, I knew better. Children are not known for being able to keep secrets, profound or mundane. If Lenny had come with us, it would be only a matter of time before he slipped and forgot his alias or mine.

I wrote out a list of items I needed Charlotte to get at the store in addition to scissors and hair dye and instructed her to get a local newspaper for job and rental hunting purposes.

I waited in the room. I was eager to explore our new town, Bay Saint Louis. I wanted to walk around outside and touch the palm trees and breathe in the salty air. I wanted to return to Beach Boulevard now that sunlight illuminated the waters, but until I looked less like me and more like Preston Myers, I was not going anywhere.

Charlotte returned from the store around three in the afternoon, and we set about making my new identity a reality. I looked into the mirror and said my farewell to the long blond hair. Charlotte would cut, dispose of the hair in the tiny trash can, and comb and cut again. The cycle continued until the length of my hair and Preston Myers was one and the same.

Next came the new color. This was my least favorite part of the process. The smell of the dye absolutely turned my stomach. I was glad when the process was complete. I could finally explore and get some much needed fresh air.

We drove across the bay to Pass Christian, Mississippi along US 90, which runs parallel the Gulf of Mexico. In all my travels across our beautiful country this stretch of road ranks right on up there in my top ten favorite roads to drive.

Grand and historic houses such as The Blue Rose and the Dixie White House line the left side of US 90- coming in from Bay Saint Louis- and the right side belongs to the Gulf of Mexico. There are convenient spots to pull off and walk along the white sand beach so we pulled over for an afternoon walk. The day had gotten away from us, having gotten up midday so we were not going to get much done by way of job hunting anyways.

The breeze was cold on my neck, and I kept trying to run my hand through my hair, forgetting I had about half as much as I was used to having. Down the beach about a ten minute walk from where we had parked, I could see the harbor, which housed a cluster of boats, and I wanted a closer look.

The berths housed a variety of boats. Some of the moored vessels were clearly used to trawl for shrimp. These dingy boats had names like My Lady Lola or Miss Daisy. Most had rust lines down their hulls. They also had large arms tied off to the boat below, and these arms reached high into the sky. The intricacy of the ropes, levers, pulleys, as the boats gently listed about in the water, held me captivated.

Others were pristinely kempt and christened Regal Red, Majestic Melody or some other name evoking an air of prestige. Most of these yachts were moored further out at the Pass Christian Yacht Club. While I was curious to see the inside of one of these decadent floating divas, the boats with a purpose, the fishing boats that put food on peoples plates and sustained the local economy, inspired me most.

The return trip to the van seemed infinitely further than the outbound portion of the walk had been, but as I have found, that always seems to be the case with trips.

We headed back to Bay Saint Louis in the hopes of locating some of the rental properties listed in the newspaper. We had to pick up a map because we got tired of having to ask the locals for directions. The first two places looked out of our price range, but the third place on Sycamore Street showed promise. It was in the one hundred block, a mere block from the bay.

We parked on the narrow street and went to get a closer look at the property. The porch was screened in, which I liked. The yard was small, but that I did not mind. We circled the house, peeking in windows to get an idea of what the inside looked like. None of the rooms were furnished, but the size and cleanliness of each seemed above par for the monthly rate of five hundred dollars plus deposit that the newspaper advertised.

We were both taken with this property and were about to leave so that we could find a phone and inquire about getting a proper walkthrough of the house, but we were stopped by one of the neighbors from across the street. He was a robust man with a full beard, booming voice, and deep accent.

"Can I hep you folks?" He asked.

We smiled, and I walked closer to greet him, my hand out-stretched in advance of my approach. Slowly he extended his hand to mine. I could tell right away that this man has labored hard all of his days. The roughness of his large and powerful hands was the tell-tale sign.

"Hi. My name is Preston Myers, and this is my fiancée, Charlotte Savoy. We saw in the newspaper that this place was for rent and were just having a look around."

"Yea, Miss Carrington passed away about two months ago, and de place been empty ever since. Lil' Ellie, uh, Ellie Bridges, is handlin' the place now. She'd be the one ya need to chat up." He continued, "My name is Jimmy Jensen. I just live across de street, over there."

Charlotte smiled and shook his hand.

"Where yall from? If I had ta guess, I'd say the lil' lady here is from New Orleans or there abouts." Charlotte nodded. "And I'd guess you from up north a piece." The man had a keen ear, and I had to admit I was impressed. My new identity dictated that I was from Texas though.

"Originally, yes. My family is from up Arkansas way, but more recently I have been living in Texas. Ever hear of Anahuac?" I prayed silently that either he had not or at the very least I was pronouncing it properly.

"Oh sure, I know it. Nice little community. Yall should fit in right nice here in Bay Saint Louis. Well, maybe we'll be neighbors. Good luck to ya. Remember, Ellie Bridges."

With that Jimmy from across the street hobbled back home. We left a few minutes later, agreeing that this was the place for us.

"He seems like a sweet old man," Charlotte remarked, waving to him as we passed.

"Yeah, but he is a sharp old bastard. Keep your guard up around him," I advised.

As soon as we returned to our room, we dialed the number in the newspaper ad, and sure enough a woman's tiny voice answered.

"This is Ellie," said the voice through the receiver.

"Yes, ma'am, my name is Charlotte Savoy, and I am calling in regards to the rental property on Sycamore

Street. My fiancée and I stopped by and had a look at it earlier and were wondering if there would be any way we could set up a time to have a look inside?"

"Sure honey. Have you got time to come by tomorrow, around noon perhaps?"

"That sounds good. We will see you then. Thanks."

We spent an hour or two doing a little online research on the town and its history before wasting away the remainder cuddled up watching cable.

Miss Bridges was waiting for us when we arrived, despite the fact that we had arrived fifteen minutes early ourselves. We played the part of the young couple, excited to be moving out on their own together, and it was easy because we were in fact, just that.

Miss Ellie, as she preferred to be called, was a sweet little gray-haired lady in her sixties. I towered over her as we stood next to her making our first formal introductions. She looked more the part of a teacher in my mind than landlord, but what did I know of what a landlord was supposed to look like? This was-hopefully going to be- my first place after all.

We stepped inside the screened porch and waited as she fumbled to unlock the front door. Her hand had a perpetual shake to it. I offered to help her, but she insisted she'd have it open in a second. As she had predicted, soon we were inside touring what we hoped would soon be our home.

This little look around was more of our chance to

get to know the owner than to decide if we wanted the place. We knew we wanted it after gazing in from the yard the day prior, but we had to know the mentality of the owner and what meddling we could expect if we moved in.

When the end of the tour came, she finally asked, "Well, darlins', what do you think?" Her hand at her side held the key, rocking with regularity back and forth.

Charlotte and I smiled to each other, silently and turned her direction. I spoke up, "We'll take it if you don't mind renting to us. I promise we won't be any trouble."

She raised her hand and made a dismissive sound. "Honey, I am a pretty good judge of character. If I thought you were gonna be trouble, I never would have let you see inside." She smiled and continued, "I'll get the rental agreement papers out of the car."

Right there, on the hood of her car, we signed the papers and paid our first month of rent and deposit. She handed us our copy of the key and told us that we could start moving in the following morning.

We were so excited as we paid for our room and headed out to move what few belongings we owned into our new home. Jimmy was sitting out on his porch and greeted us with a friendly wave as we pulled into our driveway for the first time as residents of Bay Saint Louis. I glowed inside as I thought about us becoming part of the local community. Maybe I could be what Charlotte needed and not just what she wanted. We could do this. For the first time in ages optimism gripped me.

We stepped out of the van, which had been my home for longer than had been my desire, and opened the side door.

"I see Ellie took to yall just fine. Ya need any help in with your stuff?" Jimmy offered.

"No sir, but thank you." Charlotte replied.

"Thanks for declining the help. I guess that means I get to carry most of this stuff in myself." I joked.

"Baby, I am right here by you, every step of the way."

"Well, when yall get settled in give me a holler. Would be nice to have some comp'ny round here, so maybe I can cook yall some dinner?" Jimmy said.

"Might just take you up on that, Jimmy. Thanks, but first things first." I said.

We toted the first load of stuff into the house and sat it by the front door. I was about to return for another load when Charlotte grabbed my hand. "Not so fast, Preston." She joked. "Thank you." She wrapped her arms around me and kissed me.

I smiled and said, "Charlotte, we are home, finally."

Be that as it was, we still had at least an hour of toting stuff inside and unpacking to do. "So let's get this house turned into a home."

"Okay, Preston darling."

Each time returning to the van we were greeted by the salty air. A massive tree sitting on the empty lot next to Jimmy's provided shade from the sun. Spanish moss gently swayed in the breeze overhead.

I remember wondering as we emptied the van how we ever stuffed as many things into it as we had, but I guess when you stay on the go as much as I had, you learn to make the most of every inch of given to you. If nothing else could be said of me, I knew for a fact that I was an expert at packing.

By a quarter past two we had everything inside. It was not unpacked yet, mind you, but it was inside at least. We sat on the floor, surrounded by our belongings, and pondered what to do next.

CHAPTER SIX:
A HOME OF OUR OWN

It took us a few weeks, but soon our house was indeed a home. Soon the utilities were on, and we had purchased some cheap furniture here and there. It didn't match, but it did keep us from sleeping on the floor.

We made several trips to the local Wal-Mart for food and odds and ends necessities like hangers for our clothes, light bulbs, and on and on.

Try as we might to keep to ourselves, our neighbors drew us out with their hospitality and kindness. Jimmy became our closest friend, and soon he and I were fishing together each weekend from the pier.

Every Saturday morning about eight he would come knocking on our door, fishing gear in hand. Every Saturday my response was the same, "What do you want, Old Man?" That was the term of endearment he allowed me.

His response was always the same, "Well, I got up this morning and felt like doing some charity so I figured I'd donate my time to the Teach a Yankee ta fish Foundation. You game?"

And since I never turned him down, he just kept coming around, and we grew to be damn good friends.
He invited us over to eat, and more often than not, we accepted. It did not take a genius to tell the old man was lonely and needed the company. To be perfectly honest, it was nice to be around others again. For so long I refused to make new friends, to let anyone new in. It is not the easiest thing in the world to make friends when you are wanted by the law and living life in a temporary manner.

The Old Man and I were not the only ones to grow closer. Charlotte and I talked away the nights in bed, learning infinitely more about each other. Sure Charlotte had read my book and knew about some of the things my friends and I had gone through, but I really let her in, telling her about a multitude of times left out of the book for various reasons.

She became to me what my darling Christi had once been, my other half. If I had not shared my day's happenings with her, it was as if it had not truly happened. I grew to love her, and soon the act of two people on the verge of marriage was no longer an act. She was mine, and I was hers totally.

As much as I would have loved to spend every

waking moment by her side, I knew I could not. I had to find work and provide for her. How did I do this? Did I take some grand job with endless meaning and purpose? No.

When the dust settled the only employment I could find was at the local Wal-Mart stocking dairy products. I didn't really mind it though. I usually worked from five in the morning until two in the afternoon, leaving my afternoons and evenings free to spend with Charlotte. I would never be rich from my job, but it was enough to keep the bills paid.

The days turned into months, and soon a year had passed. We had settled into our routines. Our old lives started to seem like a distant memory. I kept in touch with Mrs. Foxworth over the internet, never revealing where we were living. As far as she knew I was still living a nomadic lifestyle.

She kept me updated on little Lenny, and reassured me all the time that my decision had been the right one. I knew in my heart of hearts that it was. No matter what happened to me, a piece of Christi and I would live on through Lenny.

Charlotte used the second bedroom as a studio, painting for a few hours each day while I was at work. She painted abstracts, portraits, and landscapes, and she did all with equal ease. She supplemented our income by selling some of her paintings to a local gallery.

Bay Saint Louis had the reputation for being something of an artistic colony, and I could tell that Charlotte sincerely loved living in such a creative environment. It was a short walk to the beach, less than a block from our house, and she often watched the sunrise over the bay for inspiration.

I know what you are thinking. It sounds like the fairytale happy ending. It sounds like the story is over, and there is nothing left to tell. We both know differently though, don't we?

So when did it all fall apart? When did the dream revert to the nightmare that I thought we had escaped at long last? That is a question easily answered but extremely hard for me to write about still to this day. How could anything possibly hurt more than all the blue hues of my past? I will try my best to explain it, and maybe you will understand.

CHAPTER SEVEN:
CATASTROPHE ON THE COAST

We had been living in Bay Saint Louis for a little over two years when it happened. We thought we were going to dodge the bullet. That is what the news said. That is why we did not evacuate. That is why the end for me began on August 29th, 2005.

If that date does not mean anything to you, it should. It was on that Monday that Hurricane Katrina made landfall about ten in the morning near the mouth of the Pearl River, which is just west of Bay Saint Louis. That put us on what is considered the dirty side of the hurricane because it receives the most wind and storm surge.

Had we known this very large and powerful storm was going to shift off its expected collision course with New Orleans, we would have ran- to where

I don't really know, but we would have ran.

Jimmy had advised us that we were pretty much in the clear and a costly evacuation would be a waste of time and resources. He had lived in Bay Saint Louis for the last forty years and had seen hurricanes come and go. The last major hurricane to impact the town directly was Hurricane Camille back in 1969, and several hundreds of people lost their lives. He was fourteen at the time, and that was the only hurricane that he had ever evacuated ahead of.

Still seeing that we were nervous about riding out the category one or two winds we were expecting in Bay Saint Louis, he was gracious enough to insist we stay with him across the street until the storm passed.

The two days prior we had spent boarding up windows and securing our house and helping Old Man with his. Underneath the stilts on which his house sat he had carefully labeled boards and plywood detailing the windows for which they were cut.

The whole town was buzzing with activity. Everyone was either preparing to leave town or hunker down and ride it out. US 90 was packed with people heading to their relatives houses or other safe havens further inland.

Bay Saint Louis, I should explain, is obtainable via 43/603 south of Interstate 10, or by US 90. To leave Bay Saint Louis going east on US 90 you have to cross the Saint Louis Bay by bridge. To leave Bay Saint Louis going west on either US 90 or Interstate 10 brings you to the New Orleans area, another low-lying area. To make matters worse, the area is prone to flooding anyway, the elevation of the town is anywhere from twenty-three to twenty-five feet above sea level on average.   Old Man's house sat at about fifteen feet above sea level.

To evacuate north to Interstate 10 via 43/603 you must cross another bridge over water snaking out of the bay.   Most of the town north of US 90 has winding waterways that divide neighborhoods from each other, the people that choose to ride out hurricanes usually park their vehicles along the sides of 43/603 because the ground is slightly higher there.   For most storms, this is sufficient, but Hurricane Katrina was not your average storm.

Sunday August 28th

About four in the afternoon the day prior to the storm's arrival, Charlotte, Old Man, and I drove down to Beach Boulevard to see what Katrina was kicking our way.   The rains were starting well in advance of her arrival.   The bay's waters were unlike anything I had ever seen.   Usually the waters were calm, even at high tide, simply rising and swelling up.   On this day they seemed to be at war with the sand and piers, pummeling harshly against the coastline.

Many people were out doing the same thing we were.   The pier was full of people watching the choppy bay waters from their cars.   Few ventured out of their automobiles to brave the fierce tropical storm force winds though.

It howled outside as it pushed the van around. Ahead of us on the road I saw a truck dart off the road and into the parking lot by Saint Stanislaus, dodging the water's approach.   The waves were beginning to smash against the concrete with a thunderous roar each time, spraying and shooting water across the entire roadway.

Thinking I knew pretty well what the old van could handle, I attempted to follow the truck across the mud into the parking lot. As soon as the front tires barely made it through the mud and slowed, I knew we were stuck. I panicked and struggled to think.

Water had begun lapping at the van's passenger side. It was steadily covering more ground with each new assault. Soon the waves would be crashing down on top of us if we did not do something.

Old Man helped Charlotte out the back door, and I got out, sinking ankle-deep in mud as I did. The guys in the truck ahead had already taken notice of our predicament and were backing their truck over to us.

"We got chains if ya need a tug out."

"That'd be great!" I was exuberant that despite my ignorance, rescue was imminent. In a matter of minutes they had attached the chains and were pulling me to safety as Charlotte and Old Man watched from the safety of the parking lot.

We thanked them profusely, and, content that we had seen what we needed to see, returned home to pack up some stuff for our stay with Old Man.

That night I found myself more scared than ever before, and that is saying a lot having been a wanted man. Still I tried to keep my composure for Charlotte's sake. The last thing I wanted was for her worry to match mine.

We helped Jimmy make final preparations around the house. Cans of food and eating utensils were brought up in crates to the second floor. All windows were doubled checked and the batteries changed out in our flashlights and Old Man's weather radio. He assured us that two things were a certainty; we would lose power and there would be some flooding.

Jim showered upstairs, and insisted that we should shower as well. "Never know what the night is gonna bring. Might not get a chance to clean up again until God knows when," He said.

Charlotte and I heeded his advice and showered together. I held her close from behind, massaging her back and kissed her neck. She cocked her head to the side, offering her neck to me. We made love, cleaned up and then filled the bath tubs with clean water, our emergency drinking supply should things take a turn for the worse.

Old Man did everything he could to take our minds off the storm, feeding us an excellent home cooked meal, fixing up his spare room for us, and regaling us with tales of his years spent on the sea as a tugboat captain. Around midnight something clicked in my mind, a realization.

In the two years that we had lived in Bay Saint Louis, Jim had become something as a father figure to me. He had always been there for me, matter not the need he was always offering to fulfill it. While he was sometimes gruff with other neighbors, we always had gotten along great. He had his faults no doubt, but it was easy to see that he was a good man. I was grateful to be under his wing, out of the quickly intensifying winds and rain.

Monday August 29th

It was about two in the morning when we finally

dozed off. Charlotte and I were cuddled up in a recliner in front of the television, still tuned faithfully to the weather. Old Man had gone on up to bed on the second floor.

Every so often I would awake with a start. The winds were now howling something fierce. The massive tree that loomed over both our house and Jimmy's shook like it feared the approaching wrath of Mother Nature.

I don't remember dreaming much that night. The only dream imagery I recall was in the seconds before waking. It was Christi, my guardian angel, screaming these words, "Live! She is in danger!"

I awoke with a tremor in my soul. Everything was dark, illuminated only by the lightning outside. Thunder boomed, rumbling through me. Jim's living room was inundated with water two feet deep. I was glad the power had gone out or we would have been electrocuted for sure.

My sudden jolt back into the waking world had brought Charlotte out of her slumber as well. She clung close to me as random items from the house floated around us. The water had obliterated the door and was pouring in.

The water knocked us down as we ran for the stairs, and it was all we could do to stand let alone run against it. Somehow we finally did get upstairs. I pushed Old Man's bedroom door open and shook him back to life.

"Jim! Get up Old Man! It's happening!" I yelled.

He rubbed the sleep from his eyes. "No shit. You really woke me up when I could have slept through it?"

He asked.

"The first floor is flooding, Jim! Water is rushing in like goddamn rapids!"

I saw awareness finally kick in. His mouth dropped as he found his feet and stepped out of the room to survey the situation. Soon he was running back into his room and changing, all modesty going out the window.

The room lit completely, followed by the cracking sound of thunder and breaking glass. The whole house shook so intensely we lost our balance and fell to the floor. The consistency of the storm's clamor was like white noise eroding your nerves. It was an itch inside the mind that could not be scratched, punctuated with the sounds of the destruction of our town.

Finally we got to our feet. The three of us left his room, guided by the beam of Jim's flashlight. The water was rising with each new wave that lapped inside. It was already up nearly another half foot. Soon the whole first floor would be submerged. Jim guided us toward the second floor screened porch.

Looking back, this makes more sense to me now. Jim's porch faced north and the winds were- at that time- coming out of the southeast. The porch was somewhat shielded from the assaulting winds.

We were not particularly thrilled with going out into the storm, but it made sense to be close to an escape if the water did decide to take the house. I realized quickly that our house was probably devastated already, being one floor only and not on stilts. Everything that we had failed to bring with us from home was destroyed. Just like that every trace of our new life vanished.

The three of us ran out onto the porch. The rain was blowing sideways, judging from the angle at which it stung my face. It was a little before six in the morning, and the grating drone of the one hundred and forty mile an hour winds was maddening. Lightning struck the bending trees all around.

The whole neighborhood was under several feet of violent storm surge, and the waters showed no sign of retreating. All the trees that the winds had snapped and broken were now debris floating northwest forcefully floating and banging into houses. Personal family photos, furniture and an array of household items floated inland as well. Power lines rode the winds like copper whips ready to lash anything in reach.

Vehicles, our van included, were starting to float and bang into nearby structures. Trees were losing their branches to the powerful winds, and anything not tied down had become dangerous projectiles to be feared.

Jim assured us we would be safe on the second floor, assuming that the whole house did not float away. The storm surge was far greater than expected, but surely it had to level out soon. Unless…

It was then that we realized that we had miscalculated by not evacuating as recommended. Hurricane Katrina had shifted eastward, delivering us the full, unwanted release of her "dirty side". And we were far beyond the point that evacuation was a possibility. No emergency services were running. (I later found out that at the county courthouse everyone had written numbers on themselves in magic marker and had made a signoff sheet- which was tacked to the ceiling- to help identify the bodies if the water came much higher.) We were along for the ride, and nothing was going to change that.

The next few hours were surreal. The winds continued to howl and shift directions as the storm marched victorious over Bay Saint Louis. We braced ourselves on the porch and watched our community be overtaken by the sea continuing its rise.

By nine in the morning the Saint Louis Bay, which was usually serene, now ended a mere inch or two from the Old Man's second floor porch. The small motorboat that stayed perpetually moored off to one of the pillars supporting Jim's house collided with the structure.

"We gotta get out of here! She's still a'comin'! It's gonna wash the whole damn house out to sea!" Jim jumped for the boat and barely made it. He held on and yelled at us to follow.

Charlotte was hysterical, crying and clinging to me closer than my shadow. I knew if I jumped ahead of her she would not have the strength to follow. The boat was jostled about by the wind and waves, making the target much harder to hit.

I could see the boat sliding closer to the house and pushed Charlotte from the porch. She landed with a thud, but it was much better than landing with a splash. I stood, poised and ready, to join Charlotte and Old Man in the small craft.

Rain like I had never witnessed before began to fill the boat, helped along by the pounding waves. Charlotte was beckoning me to jump, while Jim was busy emptying bucket after bucket of water from the boat.

The last memory I have of Charlotte is her with her arm outstretched, reaching for me. As I was about to make the leap of faith into the boat, I procrastinated. I watched as a large metal sign- travelling at nearly a hundred miles an hour- sliced through Charlotte, knocking Old Man off the boat as it completed its deadly pass. Before Charlotte's body could fall what appeared to be the front door of our house knocked her into the water.

In less than a second two lives had ended, and they belonged to my two closest confidents. As much as I wanted to mourn them, instinct kicked in. I was not going to die tonight.

And what if I had? No one would have ever even known. If the tattered, out-of-date driver's license in my pocket remained, they would think that I was Preston Myers. AJ Jackson would simply become an unsolved mystery. Little Lenny would think that his daddy had just ran away and no longer cared for him. I was not going to let that happen. So I decided that mourning my losses would have to wait.

I finally did jump to the boat. I spent hours bailing water out, scanning the waters for any signs of Jimmy or Charlotte, and keeping my head down as best I could, fearing the deadly debris still being hurled about.

I wondered how long I would be out here, adrift so near to where I had lived the good life with my Charlotte for years, before help arrived. When the rain finally began to break, I sat looking at the devastation my neighborhood had endured, if that is even the proper word. Succumbed to would perhaps fit better.

The shock of all that had transpired took hold of me. I began to think about my Charlotte and Old Man floating on the violent tide, being sucked back out the the waiting sea. I began to think about all the people I had helped at work for years, and I wondered which ones left, which ones stayed, and which ones were still alive. Most of all, I wondered if this watery hell would ever subside.

CHAPTER EIGHT:
FLOTSAM AND JETSOM

As I began to think it was over, I remembered what Old Man Jim had told me about hurricanes. He had said that after the storm surge, the lull of the passing eye was one of the most dangerous things about them. It tricked people into a false sense of security. Often times people would come out of their houses to survey the damage, only to be caught unawares when the back half of the storm arrived, bringing another round of full fury.

The sun was out overhead, but all around in the distant skies loomed an ominous ring of clouds. The eye was directly overhead, signaling that this was indeed only half-time and not the end of the game. I had to prepare myself now for another assault.

I pulled the boat closer to Jim's house so that I could climb back onto the porch. I realized that after the storm passed I would be waiting a long time before help arrived. I had to find provisions enough to wait it out.

I found the food that we had brought upstairs along with the water containers we had filled up already. At least half of our water supply was still potable. The surge had leveled off, and I felt secure remaining in the house rather than returning to the boat. It was close enough to return to if the need arose, I figured.

Some of the plywood had been blown off the upstairs windows. Shards of glass peppered the floor all around. A large limb from the hulking tree outside had landed on the roof of the house. Still for all the pounding it was taking, the house was still structurally sound.

I did my best to reinforce the windows, covering them with whatever wood I could find. I could not help but pause and stare in amazement at the complete devastation. I looked down the watery canal that had been Sycamore Street, trying to remember exactly which of my neighbors had evacuated and who had chosen to stay.

Angel Delany, the single mother that lived down the street in a tiny two bedroom trailer, had stayed I was almost certain. I was pretty sure she did not have the money to evacuate. I strained my eyes to see signs of life from her trailer. What I saw simply broke my heart.

A large tree had fallen on one end of the trailer, and was probably the only thing keeping it from floating off to sea. The small vent on the top of the trailer was cranked up, the screen torn out, and a baby's arm blue and lifeless bobbed submissively adhering to the waters tug. I saw no signs of Angel, but I had to assume she had drown along with her child inside the trailer.

Across the street a man I did not recognize clung to a tree, naked except for boxers. His hair and beard matched, snow white. His body was covered with small lacerations and bruises. I yelled out to him, "Hey! Hold on, I'm coming to get you!"

I jumped back into the boat and checked the sky to see how long I had before hell was upon me once again. I figured maybe ten minutes at best so I untied the boat and started the motor.

I avoided the submerged cars and other debris as I made my way over to the man stranded in the tree. I called out to him again but still received no reply. As I got closer I realized that he had tied his hands together on the other side of the tree to hold him there against the winds. I turned off the motor and let the boat glide up next to the tree.

"Hello?" I said, starting to get a very bad feeling. I reached up to touch his shoulder. His head fell back limp. The winds must have pushed him with all of their force, probably sustained about one hundred and forty mile an hour's worth with higher gusts, into the tree. He must have suffocated under the pressure or been pummeled so hard that he bled out internally. There was nothing I could do for him. When the waters made their way back to the sea I would cut him down.

The back half of Katrina's eye was still off in the distance, so I started the motor and searched up and down the street for any possible survivors. I had to navigate with the greatest of care against all the submerged dangers hidden below the water's surface.

I yelled at the top of my lungs and hoped against hope someone out there was alive to reply. The water reeked of oil and gas amongst other things. The chemical plant across the bay, I had to assume, had flooded as well, unleashing dangerous chemicals into the flood water. Houses were half submerged as far as I could see, meaning that their toilets were all underwater as well, bringing more contamination and filth to the waters I transversed.

Dead dogs and cats that had been left by their owners floated by the boat. Near the end of our block, where the larger houses had stood across the street from the bay, now there was no trace of houses at all. Open water littered with an endless amount of building materials and bodies.

I wanted to stay out longer in the hopes that somewhere out there I would find Jimmy or Charlotte still alive, but the storm was returning to wreak more havoc.

I finally gave up and returned to the house, tying off the boat and returning to the relative comfort and safety of the dry second floor of Old Man's house. I sat down on the bed in Jimmy's bedroom, leaned back and shut my eyes. I could hear the cold water sloshing against the walls downstairs. I simply did not know what more I could do to prepare myself.

Soon the winds returns, and the sky grew dark with clouds that brought with them sideways rain and hail. It sounded as if the house was being hit with a barrage of gunfire. I felt like God himself was calling down the fury of the angels upon me. I felt like I had offended him by bringing my tainted soul to reside among the good people of Bay Saint Louis. I felt irrationally culpable.

I don't know how long the storm lasted the second time around. I spent much of it huddled in the closet inside of Old Man's bedroom. I kept my eyes on the stairs, waiting fearful that the water would rise higher and force me to flee once again to the boat outside.

A few times it got real nasty. Winds would catch the boat just right and slam it into the pillars supporting the house, causing it to shake violently. Over and over I wondered if the house had left its foundation and if I was being carried out to sea.

Windows gave way once again. Glass exploded inside. I was terrified to move. I felt an isolation I had never known before and hoped I never would have to feel again. I was all alone, surrounded above by the storm and on all sides by the sea, pissed off it had been brought along for the ride.

I had brought my laptop and a few other personal items from home and stowed them upstairs earlier. Little good would they do me now though. There was no electricity so the battery would soon die. Surely there were no communication systems up for me to secure an internet connection to get weather information. I sat clutching the Thrifty Oasis keychain while the weather radio broadcasted dead air.

At last the brunt of the storm passed, and it left in its wake the weaker tropical storm force winds and tornado spawning thunderstorms.

When the water receded and the rain ceased, I

went downstairs and shut off the main breaker. Until things dried completely I wanted to be sure the electricity would not be restored. I grabbed my pistol and stepped outside. Debris and mud covered everything. Trees and power lines were down all over the place. Every vehicle in sight was turned from where they originally were parked, often with massive amounts of debris pushed up against them. Never would these vehicles move of their own accord again.

I looked over to the body of the old man tied to the tree. I did not want others finding him that way, so I undid the knots in the rope binding him and laid him on the ground. Even though I am not a religious person, I paused to kneel and said a short prayer for him.

As I went to stand up, I slid in the rank mud. The ground was saturated, and even the slightest bit of further rain would bring a second round of flooding. I put the gun in the small of my back and went back inside to look through Jimmy's tool box. I grabbed a crowbar and went looking for survivors.

I figured going toward the bay was a lost cause and my chances were better at finding others inland, but first I wanted to check on Angel Delany and her baby. Even if they were not alive, as I feared, they should not be left inside the tattered shell of a trailer.

I pulled debris away from the trailer with the crowbar and cleared the broken glass from around a window before looking inside. Angel and her child were both dead. The mother was still in her nightgown, wet and clinging to her. Mud and muck covered much of her body. I eased her out through the window as gently as I could and laid her to rest by the old man.

It was all I could do to make myself return inside

the trailer to bring out the little girl's body, but I did. That moment has to rank right on up there with the most world changing moments one will ever experience. I was numb and felt hollow as I walked across the street, carrying a dead baby to be reunited with her mother. No words can really describe the emptiness I felt.

I laid the child across her mother's bosom and folded her arm around the kid. Again, I was compelled to say a prayer for them. While I was there, I asked forgiveness for myself as well.

For so long I had lived a life apart from the societal norm, but now I wanted to be an instrument for some greater good. And in that moment, with eyes closed and tears falling, I felt the warmth of the sun across my skin. I thought to myself that maybe this was my one chance at redemption.

The good people of Bay Saint Louis had welcomed us into their community- and homes in some cases-, and now they needed whatever help they could get. That help was going to have to initially come from within because of the scope of the disaster. The government would surely send help to the urban areas before being bothered to assist in this tiny community.

If I had survived, there had to be others, scattered and tattered and bruised, waiting for help. I would be there for them. I still could not wrap my mind around Charlotte and Old Man being truly gone from me forever. I had to find them and know for certain their fates.

CHAPTER NINE:
SEARCH AND RESCUE

I returned home and inspected the soggy remains of our house. I knew instantly that I would never live inside those four walls again. Even if it had not been destroyed, the home that Charlotte and I had made held too many memories.

Old Man's house became my camp. All my provisions were on the second floor along with my water supply. The first floor was uninhabitable and would soon be overrun with mold unless I finished the gutting that the storm had started, but first I had to help others that might not be able to help themselves.

I packed a backpack with essentials: a few bottles of water, flashlight, rounds for my pistol, a few cans of potted meat, batteries, rope, pen and notebook, and a fork. The pistol stayed in the small of my back, easily accessible, and I carried an ax that had belonged to Jimmy. If you did not know, it is common to keep an ax in the attic in flood prone areas so that you can chop your way out if the flood waters reach you. I left Old Man's house intent on finding others in need.

I searched systematically in a grid. No street signs remained, but I had a pretty good mental map of the streets after living there for so long. I started at the beach front of Sycamore, and I went house to house shouting as I walked, hoping someone would reply. At each house that I found still standing, I banged on an outside wall, waited, and then entered cautiously.

Every room, however differently laid out, always looked the same. A waterline always let you know just how deep the storm surge flooding was. Mud covered everything that was too large to float out of the house and out to sea.

Sometimes I would encounter dead pets, left when their owners evacuated because the shelters would not accept people with pets, but most bodies that I did find were pet owners who refused to leave their pets. They say you can tell a lot about a person or society by the way they treat their pets and old timers.

Many houses were completely empty. Some were not. That first day I pulled ten bodies out of various houses and to the street because it was a measure that would save search and rescue crews valuable time later on. I searched each for identification and noted their name and location in my notebook of the dead.

I had made only a few close friends since moving to Bay Saint Louis because I wanted to minimize connections. Friends are sometimes the ones that hurt you most. They know your weaknesses. Each time I brought another body out of a house and recorded what information I could find about them, I was thankful that though I might recognize the faces, I had never gotten close to them. I wondered how I would handle it if I did find Charlotte or the Old Man dead.

Don't get me wrong. I could still empathize. Each of these ended lives left behind people that cared and loved for them, and those people would hurt for a long time to come because of their passing. The best I could do was help them find closure.

By the day's end, I was getting discouraged. Here I was surrounded by corpses. I refused to believe I was the only one still drawing breath in the whole town of Bay Saint Louis. The last house I planned to check for the day sat at the intersection of Washington Street and Hancock Street.

I had always thought the house beautiful. It was pink and had a wraparound porch. It was not that it was a sprawling mansion of a house or anything. The house just seemed functional and appealing to the eye- before the hurricane anyways.

The porch had collapsed. Most of it had either blown or floated away. A waterline of about seven feet was present. I climbed through the rubble that remained and struck the ax into the roof. After a few chops, I began to notice something. There was noise coming from inside the house. Someone or something was alive inside!

I lit up. "If you can hear me, stand back! I'm gonna get you out of there!" I yelled. A muffled reply followed, which let me know that it was more than someone's pet trapped inside.

I continued to hack away. Eventually I removed enough of the roof's corner for the inhabitants to escape. As I pulled the boards away to make more room, I talked to the people inside and discovered that a family of three was all alive and well, but they had become trapped from the swelling of the wood around their exit door.

A woman in her thirties was the first to climb out of the attic hole. Her six year old daughter followed next, and at last the patriarch of the family joined us in the dying sunlight and shook my hand.

The coup of finding survivors reinvigorated me, and I would have continued my search into the night save for the fact that these people needed me still. Their house was in ruins, and I was not about to have them stay in their attic. I led them back to Old Man's house for some food, water, and company; all were things I needed as badly as they did.

The walk back was not far, but as the sun sank closer to the horizon the dangers increased. Wild animals from further out had been pushed in with the waters. Snakes were everywhere. Power lines were down, some still very much live. Boards with nails awaited the unsuspecting foot.

I led the way with the flashlight, the lady behind me and the father brought up the rear toting his daughter. When we neared Jimmy's, I made a point to alter our route enough that the women would not see the three bodies across the street.

Soon we were inside and able to rest in relative comfort. It was nice to get away from all the disgusting mud and filth. I got them each a bottle of water and a few cans of food before stepping out onto the porch to wash my hands over the side. I had been hauling dead bodies out all day and playing in the rank mud and wanted no part of illness in these conditions.

We sat on the floor in a circle and talked while we ate. I gave them my alias and fictional background, and they told me about their family.

His name was Ryan Rankin, and he was a mechanic. He was originally from Iowa but had moved his family down to Bay Saint Louis only a month or so back. He seemed like a good man. He was bigger than me and had piercing eyes. He possessed the type of voice that people listen to, as he reserved his words for times when they were needed most and stayed silent the rest of the time.

His wife's name was Sloan. She looked to be about five or six years younger than her husband. She had beautiful straight blond hair. Her eyes were as blue as the bay waters usually were, and her smile lines told the story of a woman who was always in good spirits.

Their daughter, Katelynne, was very shaken up. The fresh memories of the storm didn't seem to have faded from her sharp little mind yet. Her hair was also blond, but given to curling on the ends. She was the perfect picture of innocence.

When we finished eating and talking I tried the weather radio again. After some searching on the AM band, I finally found news. It was a radio station broadcasting out of New Orleans, and the news it brought did nothing to lighten our spirits.

While New Orleans had escaped the brunt of Hurricane Katrina's wrath, they had major issues in the city. Some of the levees had been breached. The city was flooded in parts and the loss of life was massive. My heart wept for the city of New Orleans, but at the same time I knew that a disaster of that magnitude would slow help getting to all of the outlying areas. We were going to be on our own for a long time to come.

I had to start thinking more long term. The food and water that was in my possession was not going to last more than a couple of days, and I realized that it might be weeks before help arrived. I still planned on searching out and helping as many people as I was able to, but with each additional survivor the resources would grow scarcer.

I gathered some bedding materials and made a pallet for myself on the floor and insisted that Ryan and his family take the bed. They politely declined at first, but I insisted. I was not ready to turn in yet.

In fact, there was still more work to be done. I knew exactly which houses that I had removed the dead from earlier, and I also knew which of those houses I had found cans of food in earlier. I needed to retrieve them and build our pantry for the long road to recovery we would soon find ourselves walking.

With no shelters yet set up that I knew of in Bay Saint Louis, I felt no remorse looting the supplies we needed since I knew the owners would not be needing them. Let's face facts; years on the run had lowered my morals in that I had no compunction about stealing when it came to what I considered vital needs.

I loaded a pistol and left it with Ryan. I wanted

to be sure they would be safe in my absence. The other pistol remained with me. I told them I was going out to look for food, and I would return in an hour or two. Darkness like few ever get to see greeted me outside. You don't realize just how much light our cities emit until they go dark.

Flashlight illuminating the way through the muddy streets I retraced my earlier route, cleaning out any can food products that I came across. Any other valuables I left where I found them. I had no need for them or the desire to take them.

I made several trips back to the house to unload my pack. I shined the light all around while I walked. There was no telling what you would find on the ground, left abandoned by the waters. All I could think as I walked around was that these items were all pieces of people's lives.

They had worked away years of their lives to accumulate all this shit, and in one day's time Katrina had taken it all from them. Their years of hard labor had been in vain, and I wondered if they realized that their true wealth was the time they spent with their families.

Even after moving to Bay Saint Louis Charlotte and I had maintained our Spartan lifestyle. We purchased only to meet our needs, rarely our wants. But just as with everyone else, Katrina managed to take away my everything, my Charlotte. At least little Lenny was not with me. He was safely out of harm's way.

One of the few creature comforts I had allowed myself was an iPod that I had bought to listen to music while I stocked milk in the dairy cooler at work. It held about a thousand of my favorite songs. I put on Simon and Garfunkel's "America" and stuffed the buds into my ears. The melody started with its familiar soothing humming and I continued my final hike of the night back to Old Man's house.

The words snaked into my brain, "I'm empty and aching, and I don't know why…" But I did know why. I walked and gently sobbed to myself. My back was beginning to ache from all of the straining and pulling and toting. Luckily I was approaching the house.

I wiped my tears away, turned off the iPod to conserve precious battery power, and brought the last load of food up to the second floor. I tried to be as quiet as possible so I would not disturb my guests.

Despite my best efforts at stealth and silence, I still woke Ryan. "It's just me, Ryan." I reassured him in the darkness.

"Preston, thanks for everything."

"Don't mention it. Get some rest. It is going to be a long day tomorrow." I replied.

I took a towel and went out on to the porch alone and cleaned up as best I could. With water scarce, I used only enough to wet an end of the towel and scrub away the dried mud. The sea salts and chemicals in it burned my skin and left it irritated and red.

I changed into one of the few clean pair of pants I had and found my pallet. I put my pistol under the pillow as was always my custom, and no sooner than my head hit the pillow, sleep was upon me. No dreams. No laying awake worrying. Exhaustion in its purest form simply flipped a switch inside, and I was out.

Tuesday August 30th

I woke around seven in the morning. My body ached, and the world seemed muffled. Every sound you are so used to hearing, I still heard, but at a distance. Prolonged exposure to the wind and accompanying noise had dulled my hearing.

I wanted to lay there as long as I could without facing another trying day, but with each minute that passed I felt guiltier for delaying. I had air in my lungs. So many people I had known no longer did. Maybe Old Man and Charlotte were among them. I drug myself up and off my pallet.

I rummaged around the food we had amassed and decided on fruit cocktail for breakfast. Then, I filled two water bottles and walked out on the porch. Ryan and his family were still asleep, so I left them be.

I flipped a five gallon bucket over for a seat and ate my breakfast. The air outside had grown fouler overnight. The heat had intensified, drying the mud to an oily consistency. And as it dried, it stank more and more like the rankest vomit you ever smelled. Dead things, people and animals alike, rotted in the heat. Our once beautiful beach front community had become a post-apocalyptic hell.

Though my hearing was not perfect, I detected a distant humming, and it was growing louder. I turned up the rest of my canned breakfast and grabbed my water and gear. In a flash I was out of the house and bolting down Sycamore toward the beach. Reflexes quicker than ever, I dodged a million hazards with easy, inspired by the sound of approaching helicopters.

Help was on the way! I arrived in the freshly cleared area facing the beach, surrounded only by rubble and empty foundations and spotted six military helicopters flying in formation directly towards me. The government was going to take care of us after all. I waved my arms frantically to get their attention. They were flying so low I even made eye contact with one of the pilots, and he returned my wave. That was right before they left me amongst a cloud of blowing dirt, sand, and debris.

Pallets of bottled water and supplies dangled below them as they grew smaller once again, heading surely to New Orleans. Those were the first helicopters to fly over, as if teasing us with aid meant not for us, but they were by no means the last. As the day wore on I counted at least thirty more that came from nearby Kessler Air Force Base and went leaving Bay Saint Louis no better than they found it.

Let me pose a few rational questions for all of you reading out there. Indulge me. Would it not make more sense from a purely logistical standpoint for the government to dispense supplies to those towns in closest proximity to the bases and then work their way out further? Would aid not reach more communities quicker? Were we any less American citizens than those needy New Orleanians?

Because the contraversy regarding the flooding in New Orleans had become an even bigger media shit storm than Katrina, it was going to be just as I had feared. We were being relegated to a position of low-priority in the wake of New Orleans's failing levees.

CHAPTER TEN:
COME TOGETHER

Over the next few days I continued my search and rescues. I enlisted Ryan's help. We worked out a pretty good system. We each used a spray paint of different colors to mark the structures we had searched. We marked each house denoting if there were dead inside. When we found clean food, we took it. When we found anything that might benefit the group as a whole, such as tarps or tools, we took it.

Soon we had added many survivors to our ranks. In the first day or two we had added ten people to our growing family. Jim's house was turning into an unofficial shelter, but with no real shelters open yet we did the best we could. We had very little by way of first aid supplies, and what we did have went very quickly. Injuries abounded.

The most common injury I noticed was raw hands from where people had gripped whatever was in reach and held on for dear life. It took the hurricane's eye nearly twelve hours to clear Bay Saint Louis. Imagine having to hold on to something with all of your might for that long.

Bloody and blistered, battered and bruised, mourning and confused were those we took in. So many had lost loved ones either by separation or death, and their eyes always had the same distant stare. While we managed to scavenge food enough, water for drinking and keeping wounds clean was a different story. Each bottle of water that we found was a blessing.

I would be lying if I was to say that I remember the names of everyone that joined us at Jim's, but most of their faces have remained embedded in my mind. Three of the survivors that I found I remember well though. Their names were Kristine, Alaina, and Kevin, and I found them rummaging through what was left of Kristine's house.

Kristine and Kevin Patterson were brother and sister. She looked to be about twenty three and had shoulder length blond hair. She seemed to be coping well, all things considered, as she collected what keepsakes remained.

Kevin was older than Kristine by about five

years. He was lean and lanky and sounded more southern than his sister when he talked. I soon learned of his background in firefighting and emergency first aid. In the days to come he assumed the unofficial role as our doctor.

The young girl that accompanied them barely looked eighteen. She was pale, abnormally so. Her curly black hair and black lipstick contrasted her complexion. What makeup she was wearing when the storm came through lingered like dried black tear stains down her cheeks. She looked like a straight up gothic mess when I first met her. It soon became clear that Alaina was Kristine's better half.

The four of us soon became pretty good friends. Along with Ryan and Sloan they kind of took on a senior management role helping keep order within our growing household.

Thursday, September 8th

Ten days after the storm our shelter housed nearly thirty people, all on the second floor of Old Man's house. Even as I had searched day after day for them, I had still found no sign of either Charlotte or Old Man. News continued to filter in from New Orleans and the surrounding cities, most of it bad.

Ryan, Kevin, and were out looking for others just south of US 90 when we finally started running into groups of survivors and people trying to return home. I knew that some of these people had not stayed through the storm because they had functioning vehicles.

Several SUV's were parked in front of Bay Elementary School, and they were unloading supplies. I approached the group of people doing the unloading and asked what was going on. At last a shelter was being set up locally.

It was more appropriately called a POD, or Point of Distribution center, but across the street was a clearing. People were already in the process of setting up tents and other makeshift shelters from the sun and heat.

We offered our assistance unloading the food, water, and medical supplies, and it was gladly accepted. We talked as we worked and learned that this was only the initial shipment of many to come. Locals with no place to go were being invited to post up across the street.

Finally we had a place for our people so they would not all be crowded inside of Old Man's house. It was not that I minded them being there, but it was becoming more of a hazard every day. Mold was starting to form downstairs. People were crowded in close quarters, many with infections trying to set in. It was time to turn them over to people better trained to help.

Back at Jim's I shared the good news that people were finally getting organized to help get our community back on its feet. We packed up our gear and began our more or less single file exodus march to Bay Elementary School. Those that were too sick or unable to walk the eleven blocks remained at Jim's until I could arrange transportation for them to the shelter.

I figured it would be easy to get someone to drive them over to the school, but gas was scarce with Katrina having knocked out so much of the refining and distribution systems for the oil industry. Those who were lucky enough to have gas were hoarding their supply to keep them mobile and run their generators.

These people were not my family, but they might have well been. I was not going to leave them behind. I enlisted the help of Ryan, Kevin, and another stout fellow to go get them. We had to take down four of Jimmy's interior doors to double as stretchers. Two men to a door we made three trips, eleven blocks each way, to get all eight of the infirm to the shelter where food and water were more abundant.

Afterwards we found ourselves setting up lean-to's and tents for these same people. By the time I got around to setting up my own tent, darkness had come. I slept filthy that night and could not have cared less. Every bone in my body ached profusely, but I went to sleep with a smile on my face. Each one of those aches and pains was born out of my desire to not only survive but also to help my neighbors, and it was the most rewarding feeling I have ever experienced.

Friday, September 9th

The next day I did not work outside of the shelter. I was exhausted emotionally and physically. Instead I remained at the school, helping those in charge set up the Point of Distribution. I unloaded goods that had started pouring in from across the nation. I helped sort them. I set up all of the medical supplies in the back corner and acted as pharmacist for part of the day, dispensing bandages, peroxide, hand sanitizer, aspirin, and the likes.

Most of the people were pretty easy going, but you always have some people who want to over-exert their authority. I am not going to get into all of that though because so many good people did so much to help selflessly in our time of need. It would take away from the accomplishments of the many to focus on the obstacles erected by the few.

I remember the day most because it was the first time in two weeks that I recall seeing people laugh and smile. It did not happen often, but when it did it gave me hope. Things were going to get better.

Saturday, September 10th

I spent most of Saturday helping drag debris out of the road so relief supply trucks had more routes open to the shelter. We cleared residential streets too so that those too stubborn to leave their molding abodes could benefit from the door to door efforts of churches and other philanthropic organizations handing out bibles and hot meals.

While I am talking about them I must confess that it always bothered me that they would use a person's darkest hour as a chance to convert. If people need food and you want to do good and provide what you are able to for them, you should not attach strings to the offer. You should give it expecting nothing back, even if all you expect is one's time and attention or to take the offered gift of a bible. It is just my opinion on the matter, but it is something that I feel very strongly about.

Since we had grown closer over the last two weeks, Ryan and Kevin and I continued to work together. We had forged a bond and made a very efficient team. We even set up our camps side by side, and every evening we would eat our meals together around a common campfire.

Sloan kept Katie during the day while she helped out in the school. Kristine sometimes joined us guys chopping up fallen trees, clearing roads, and helping people gut their houses while Alaina helped at the shelter. Everyone contributed something to the betterment of the group according to their means.

Around the campfire we shared much about ourselves. Kristine told about how she had met Alaina while working as a substitute teacher. Alaina would always ask for help so Kristine would lean over her, putting her breasts in her face. More than once Kristine noticed that Alaina had hiked her skirt high up on her thighs trying to get the attention that Kristine was more than glad to give.

Kevin shared how he always knew that Kristine swung both ways, but he never could prove it. That is, until he saw her kissing Alaina last New Year's Eve at one of the local bars.

Ryan and Sloan also spoke of how they met. I guess it just helped us to cope with things talking about the better times, forgetting for the moment the trials of the day. They had worked together at the local cinema up north in their hometown.

Ryan told us what a fool he made of himself every time Sloan was near. He had been- by his own account- desperate to be noticed by her. The first day he met her was at an employee meeting when she came in dressed to the nines. "Picture it, there she was dressed in a tight black dress looking like a young Gwyneth Paltrow, and then there was me, dorky as hell back then, following her around like a little puppy dog." He pulled her close and kissed her and said, "But somehow she did notice me, and the rest is history."

We all went silent. The fire crackled in front of us, and I knew they wanted me to tell them more about my life before Katrina had come along. I told them about Old Man and Charlotte, and how I missed them so. I told them about Charlotte and her amazing ability to paint and draw. I told them about Jimmy and the crazy shit he would talk about while we fished off the pier. I told them just enough to paint the portrait of a boring, heartbroken average Joe, but no more. Only Kevin persisted.

"Did you grow up here?" He inquired.

"No, Texas."

"Your accent doesn't really say Texas to me. You sound more like a Yankee to me. I would have guessed Saint Louis." He added.

He had me rattled. I didn't know what to say, so I simply said goodnight and retired for the evening, and as I sprawled out inside of my tent I cried. I missed my Charlotte. I missed cuddling up next to her. I missed posing for her so she could paint me. I even missed the rare occasion when we would argue.

Finally, as if an angel had watched me lay there in torment, sleep saved me. I dreamed of JP that night, and that he and Mr. Fields had never fought. I dreamed of the alternate course all of our lives would have taken had it never occurred. It was a divine distraction while it lasted, but in the morning I found myself saddened by the return to reality.

CHAPTER ELEVEN: REINTRODUCTION

Sunday, September 11th

The next day marked ten years of living on the run, hiding from the law. Those days spent on the road seemed like distant memories given the present state of things. I felt like a different person. There I was contributing to community in the best way that I could. I had a job. I had a home. I had Charlotte. That was before Katrina took everything.

After Katrina, I had nothing and no interpersonal relationships that had lasted longer than the last few weeks. I was surrounded by people from my adopted town and volunteers that had started arriving from around the world, but I felt alien and out of place.

I worried less about being discovered though. The more I thought about it, the more secure I felt. Everyone was in survival mode. No one was even thinking about pre-Katrina trespasses. People coming in would tell us of driving over one hundred miles an hour down I-10 and cops not even batting an eye. One of the few convenience stores open only allowed five customers in at a time and didn't card for beer or cigarettes. Many volunteers brought weed with them and smoked it freely around the fire at night. We were living on the outskirts of civilized society, and as long as you did not venture out past the twilight curfew imposed by the military you could get away with just about anything.

Each day several lists were maintained and updated at the shelter. One for people requesting assistance clearing debris from their yard, getting trees off their roofs and tarps on them, and gutting their houses. One that kept track of all survivors staying on the school grounds, and one that listed all of the dead that had been identified and a number of John and Jane Does waiting to be identified. I checked the lists daily and prayed I would not find Charlotte or Old Man listed under fatalities.

I crawled out of my tent and pulled my combat boots on. I was still filthy from yesterday, but I saw no reason to take a cold shower before going right back out to get dirty so I skipped it. I went into the school and helped myself to an MRE (Military Meals Read-to-Eat) for breakfast.

Most people who have eaten MRE's will tell you that they are horrible, but I disagree. They beat canned foods in my mind. The one I ate for breakfast was labeled *Pork Rib, Boneless in BBQ*, and it hit the spot. The food is designed to be eaten straight out of the pouches or heated by the included chemical stove that boils water without a fire.

In the days that followed the military brought in a veritable smorgasbord of MRE entrees. I think I counted somewhere around forty different meal selections. The only one that I could not stomach was the *Scrambled Eggs*.

After breakfast one of the coordinators asked if I would help a crew going down to Ballentine Street. Someone had noticed a more pronounced smell of death in the area and asked if we could sift through the debris and retrieve any bodies. I agreed to help complete the gruesome chore.

We spent hours digging around on the one hundred block guided by our noses and instincts. When the surge receded, it did so to the southeast after having pushed in from the same direction.

In the first two hours we found three bodies, two male and one female. I did not personally dig any of the three out. They were discovered first by other volunteers. Kevin uncovered one of the male corpses. All were discovered face down.

My heart sank and my stomach turned. Two weeks of putrefaction is not a pretty sight. The bodies were bloated and discolored purple in places where the blood had settled. The extra fluid build up in the corpses coupled with the humidity had accelerated the decomposition something fierce.

We gathered around, as close as we dared knowing what our stomachs could handle, and watched as Kevin put on his rubber gloves and searched the pockets for any clue as to the identities of these poor souls. He found nothing on the first male, but as he rolled him over I lost everything my stomach had to give. It was Old Man. The sea he loved so much had claimed his life. As much as the revelation saddened me, I could not take my eyes off the female corpse. *Is it Charlotte?* Same complexion. Same color hair. I was compelled beyond reason to end my unknowing.

I climbed over to the body and grabbed a hold of it without any gloves and turned her over. The stench worsened as I moved the body and gases expelled themselves from the body's rotting insides. The blank face staring back at me was not Charlotte.

All the volunteers watched in horror, sympathetic to my aching heart. I let the tears fall. My hands I held out and away and climbed back off the rubble. As I passed Old Man's body I spoke up, "His name was Jimmy Jensen. It was his house I took you to." An insect crawled out of his thick white beard. "He was my friend." I hung my head and started to walk solemnly back to Bay Elementary alone.

The roads all looked more like narrow alleys with all the dirt and drying mud covering them. In the distance I could hear crews working to clear yards and gut houses. The stench of corpses was in my clothes and on my skin. I could not escape it.

When I returned to the shelter I noticed more new volunteers arriving, but I only wanted to remove the smell of death from my person and retire to my tent. I grabbed some hand sanitizer and other personal hygiene items from inside the shelter and headed for a secluded place to clean up.

I did not come out of my tent for the rest of the afternoon or even later that night. I did not sleep. Instead, I lay there dazed and confused. I listened to the voices of my camp mates talking and heard the noises of their comings and goings. They seemed to walk on eggshells and fall silent whenever they would pass my tent. Someone new had joined out encampment. I knew because there was another voice I could not place right away, but eventually I knew it too.

As I listened to the voice of the newcomer, I knew I had heard it before, but from where I could not place it. Eventually the question arose as to where this do-gooder haled from, and, "Dexter, Missouri," was the reply. "It's a small town you probably never heard of," said the stranger.

It was Sloan that spoke up, "Wasn't that where the Brat Pack was from?" She looked around and found a few in camp staring blankly back at her. "Oh come on, you have to remember that. They killed a bus driver and took off across the country robbing and killing. What was the leader's name again?"

"AJ Jackson," said the mystery voice.

"Did you know him?" Sloan inquired.

"Kinda. We went to school together."

You have got to be fucking kidding me! I come all

this way, so many years later and run into someone that I went to school with!

I sat silent, hanging on every word. I did not dare to inject myself into the conversation or leave the tent.

Sloan was intrigued, "What was he like? I mean, were there any signs he was dangerous?"

The voice laughed. "No, not really. He seemed as normal as the next kid. We had a few classes together. He was smart. He never seemed to pay attention though. He was too busy writing poetry, but somehow he always managed to pull off the grades."

Kevin, who had been silent up until now, asked, "Do you think he did all those things they say he did?"

"Well, I read his book. So I have heard his version of things as well as what all the news reports had about it on television. The full truth probably lies somewhere in between."

I had to have a look and see who this guy was. I still could not place the voice and it was killing me. I stood up inside the tent and peeked out the ventilation mesh. Illuminated only by the light of the fire, shadows dancing across them all, I finally made the connection. He was Court Donnelly. Shawn was his cousin.

We were never really close enough that I would have called him a friend, but by the same token we had never been at odds either. How would he react if he did remember me?

I wondered if he would recognize me if he saw me. I am not so sure that I would have recognized him on sight alone by the light of day. Ten years had passed after all. He had put on some weight, carrying most of it in his beer gut. His brown hair was longer than I remembered it, and his left cheek had been scarred by fire.

I lay back down and tried to calculate the odds of running into someone from my past with so much time and distance separating us. The only conclusion I could come to was: Astronomical.

Monday, September 12th

Despite the sun turning the interior of my tent into an easybake oven, I did not want to leave it come morning. Court was there running around somewhere, and I was still scared of having my true identity exposed. Having lost everything else, my alter-ego as Preston Myers was all I had left. Still, I could not hide inside my tent forever.

I decided to distance myself from the group a bit and work on fixing Old Man's house. It was the closest thing to a home that I had. I had no idea how long Court would be volunteering out of Bay Elementary, and I really did not want to chance him recognizing me. If I moved back into Old Man's house and spent my days gutting it and renovating it I would have sanctuary. Sure adjusters and city officials would probably come around and hinder my renovating, but the main objective was to get the deadly mold out of the interior.

I waited out my camp mates and came out of hiding only after they had all left to do another hard day of volunteering. While they were gone, I took down my tent, collected my belongings, grabbed as much food and water as my bag would hold, and hoofed it back to Jimmy's.

I was furious when I reached the second floor. Looters had picked through nearly everything Old Man had owned. I was thankful they had not found his tools.

I sat down on the bed and mulled over where I was going to start amongst other things. I thought about Jimmy. Never again would he sleep on that bed or look on the framed photos around the room, reminded of fond memories. His life was over like so many other people I had left in my wake.

I had to move and get my mind working on something menial and gutting houses was perfect for that. I grabbed my trusty crowbar, a hammer, and a shovel and went to work on the living room. I moved everything that was waterlogged inside out to the edge of the yard. A few sticks of furniture were salvageable so I moved them upstairs.

All of the drywall below the waterline had to come out. If the waterline was in the middle of a sheet, the whole sheet would have to go. I didn't have a mask of any kind, so I was taking a huge risk to my health breathing in the mold.

For hours I laid into the drywall, exercising demons and letting all of my frustration out on the house whose owner I missed greatly. The heat was miserable. The cuts and scrapes I had accumulated living in the affected zone and trying to help out all cried out as my sweat stung them.

The beating the shit out of the walls part went

fast, but I could not find a wheel barrel so each load of debris I carried by hand out to the ever-growing trash heap. I tried to pace myself and remember to rehydrate often. As the drywall was removed, it became apparent to me that the insulation underneath would have to go as well.

The fiberglass particles got on my skin and made me itch something awful. The living room was almost done, but I needed to rest. It was time for a lunch break I figured.

I grabbed a MRE and a bottle of water and made my way up to the second floor porch to eat. I felt at home there. Jimmy and I had snacked many times there, but the food he cooked was always significantly tastier than your average MRE.

Old Man could sure make a mean seafood gumbo, and his company always soothed me. I never felt like I was working at guarding my secrets with him. He didn't pry into my past. He had seemed happy enough just having someone to spend time with. He had adopted me more or less. And now, here I was resting between bouts of demolishing the mold infested first floor of his house while his remains were being reclaimed.

I poured the water into the chemical stove, dropped in the food packet, stuffed the open edge back into the cardboard container, and leaned it against my chair to cook for a few minutes. The meal was not exactly gourmet, but it was the fuel I needed to keep going.

After eating, I leaned my head back and closed

my eyes. The sun was bright out, and I was thankful for the shaded porch.

I was nearly nodding off when I heard the honk of a car approaching. Kevin leaned out of the passenger side window and yelled, "Hey bubba, how you holding up?"

I said nothing, but nodded my head.

"Yeah, that's what I though." The driver turned off the car, and Kevin and company got out. Ryan was with him, but he was not the one driving. "We heard you left camp. Figured we would find you here." He looked over to the trash heap. "Looks like you been busy guttin' today."

"Yeah, Old Man is gone, but maybe I can save his house. Gotta get the mold out." I replied.

"Sounds like a plan." He called back for the driver to pop the trunk. "Well, I never met the Old Man, but if he was a friend of yours he must have been one hell of a fella."

"He was. I would not be here today if he had not invited Char…" I could not even say her name.

Kevin could sense my pain. He was already on his way up to me, followed by Ryan. The driver remained downstairs.

After a long pep talk I followed them downstairs, agreeing to let them help me gut the first floor. I really wanted to be alone, but I could tell they were not going to be dissuaded.

CHAPTER TWELVE:
HOW'S IT GOING TO BE?

The driver, I soon realized, was Court Donnelly. I also realized I had agreed myself into another fine mess. I had no idea how I was going to get out of this one if he recognized me.

Kevin made the introductions between Court and me. I shook his hand and detected a slight pause in our handshake, a tale-tell sign of recognition. I tried to play it cool and went right to work. The less I spoke, the better I felt.

We had all been doing this kind of relief work

for awhile now, so I figured no one needed any guidance from me. We knocked out walls, down to the beams and studs, and carried our mess outside. Once in awhile I would catch Court glancing my way, as if trying to work out the same puzzle in his mind I had been working on last night.

I found myself silently praying that my disguise would hold up to his scrutiny. The others conversed while they worked, talking about their lives before Katrina. Eventually, Ryan asked Court, "What do you back in the real world?"

I was about to swing the crowbar to knock off another section of drywall, but I steadied myself long enough to hear his answer.

"I am police officer," he replied, looking straight at me. "I work for the Dexter Police Department."

Kevin chimed in about the experience he had working as a firefighter and EMT. Court kept up his end of the banter, but was clearly paying more attention to my actions than Kevin's words.

"What got you interested in law enforcement?" Kevin asked.

"Well, you remember that conversation we had last night, about the Brat Pack?" The guys nodded, and Court continued, "My cousin is Shawn Wilson. He was friends with AJ Jackson and several of the others that helped kill that bus driver."

The room was silent. All tools had stopped their work, and all I could do was look at the floor as he talked. "Shawn didn't really play a part in all of it, but because he fled the scene with them he did five years in prison. He came out changed. Prison really messed him up, derailed his whole life. I always hoped I might pull over AJ on a routine traffic stop and bring him in, for what he did to Shawn."

"Damn, that's messed up! You think you'll ever find him? That was a long time ago. Hell, he could be dead by now." Kevin said.

"I used to think that too, but something tells me he is still out there somewhere. He has probably lived a better life than Shawn has since his release." He cut his eyes at me again. "His day in court is coming."

I stepped outside with my warming bottle of water and sat down. They all followed me outside. All I wanted was a few minutes to collect my thoughts and process what the hell to do next. I had to get some distance between Court and me, but how? I had no vehicle. Curfew would be setting in soon. I had yet to find Charlotte's remains, something I needed for closure. Where would I run?

"Guys, if ya'll excuse me for a few, I'm gonna walk down to the bay for a minute. I'll be back in a few." I stood and had taken about five steps when I heard a clicking sound behind me. It was a sound I knew well. There was a loaded gun cocked and pointed at the back of my head.

"I am afraid I can't let you wonder off, Preston. I think you know why." Court said.

I had my back to Kevin and Ryan so I couldn't really see their reactions, only hear their words.

"What the hell are you doing?" Kevin screamed at Court.

"Turn around and keep your hands high. You want to tell them, Preston, or should I?" Court threw a pair of handcuffs at me that I dared not move suddenly to try to catch. They hit me in the chest and fell to the muck-laden ground.

I considered trying to bullshit my way out of it, but if push had come to shove, which it would have, my fingerprints would have proved me the liar that I was. *So this is how it all ends, huh?*

"Lean over and put em' on, slowly." He demanded.

"Preston, what the hell?" Ryan begged.

"It is true…" I eased down to grab the cuffs. "I am not Preston Myers." *Click.* "I am AJ Jackson." *Click.*

From that point on, Court and I were joined at the hip. He kept his gun trained on me, almost daring me to try to escape. The look in his eyes told me that he would not hesitate to shoot me. He was far from his jurisdiction, but I knew better than to think that would stop him.

Everyone was dumbfounded when we arrived back at the shelter. Here I was, one of Bay Saint Louis's own model citizens, making my walk of shame in front of everyone. A crowd began to form around us, faces exhausted from another hard day's work and perplexed as to how I had come to return in handcuffs.

"Everybody stay back! This is not Preston Myers!" Court shouted. He pointed to one of the sweet old ladies who had organized the shelter and yelled,

"Get me the sheriff, and tell him I am making a citizen's arrest of one, AJ Jackson."

Lawdog was having his moment, just the way he had dreamt it would be for so long, and then a funny thing happened. The crowd tightened around us, despite Court's continued admonishments to stay back.

To these people I was not AJ Jackson, fugitive. To these people I was neighbor, friend, volunteer, and in some cases rescuer. I had earned their respect, and I still had it, despite having trampled all over their trust.

Ryan and Kevin eased in closer behind Court and disarmed him. Through the crowd, down low, I saw Katelynne pushing her way through to get to me. She hugged my waist though I could not hug her back. In the sweetest voice that I have ever heard she said, "Thank you for saving us." Afterwards she ran back to her mommy and daddy.

Ryan tossed Sloan the keys to the handcuffs, and she removed them from me. Ryan motioned to her, and she took the cuffs to her husband. Soon Court was cuffed to a nearby bike stand.

Ryan leaned close to me and whispered, "Look, you may have lied to us about who you really are, but that does not change the fact that you saved me and my family. You saved half the people staying here. Now we are saving you." I was touched.

I looked at him, full of gratitude. Maybe an angel was looking over me. Who knows, maybe Christi or Charlotte? "Here are his car keys. Take them and get as far away as you can."

I shook his hand, and then Kevin's, followed by

what felt like thousands. I stopped by Old Man's house one last time to retrieve what few supplies and belongings I still had, and once again I hit the open road.

As I drove I prepared myself mentally for the stresses of a return to a way of life I thought I had left behind me. I prepared myself for a return to the ways of a person I had not been in over a year. I prepared myself for a life lived alone. It would be better that way because I was filled to the brim with a decade's worth of hurt and loss. I needed no more.

As it turns out, I would need the preparations, just not in the capacity I expected. I drove east on I-10, and within an hour I arrived at a military checkpoint…after curfew. When they had me exit the car, I knew I was experiencing my last few moments of freedom for years and years to come.

CHAPTER THIRTEEN:
WHERE HAVE ALL THE CRIMINALS GONE?

I will not bore you with the tedious details of the trial and transport to prison or the time I spent in classification. Suffice it to say that all of my good deeds as Preston Myers did nothing in the eyes of the law to alleviate my culpability in all the crimes we committed or was accused of having committed.

I was convicted of multiple felonies including arson, aiding and abetting, identity theft, several counts of evading law enforcement, and several other trumped up charges. I was accused of armed robbery and home invasion, and both charges were complete and total bullshit.

Despite my original crimes being committed in Missouri, I was sentenced to FCC Pollack in the town of the same name in Louisiana. The length of my sentence was to be no more than twenty years and no less than eight years.

Friday, June 2nd, 2006

My senses were overloaded that first day in general population with so much information to process. There I was in a new environment with over thirteen hundred other inmates, mostly violent offenders, and I had only myself to blame. There were new rules to learn. There was a new society to adapt into, and something told me that the learning curve was going to be steep. I would have to learn fast.

I had been issued seven of each articles of clothing stenciled with an eight digit inmate registration number (30446-573). This number was also linked to my commissary fund account. Now that I was assigned to maximum security, I was also given an inmate identification card and one mean-as-fuck looking cellmate.

He was covered in tattoos. One tattoo across his forearm had his name, Nick, elaborately displayed, and when it was flipped it read, Katie. I soon found out that was his woman's name.

He had short brown hair and a goatee that refused to fill in completely. He was twenty-five and much larger than me. We said very little that first night, only briefly acknowledging each other. Plenty of time to get to know each other, but at the time I just wanted to sleep.

The hurry up and wait mentality that guided the processing of new inmates really frustrated me and wore me out. All my life I had done what I wanted when I wanted to do it, but those days were over. I was on prison time. My every waking second was a pie that the BOP (Bureau of Prisons) got to slice according to their whims and fancies.

About the time I was dozing off I heard someone shout, "Count!" I heard our cell door release and watched my cellie step out onto the yellow line holding his identification card. I hopped off the top bunk and followed suit.

Guards were making their rounds on each tier, matching the faces on their clipboards to the ones on our identification cards. We were each told to say our number and did so.

As the two guards on our tier passed, I watched, fascinated at how smoothly the routine worked when everyone was in compliance. I read their names from their uniforms, Officers Broussard and Long.

They both were big men, fitting the role of eighties wrestler that went by the name of Big Boss Man. Broussard was black with hair shaved close, and his uniform had sharp creases. He wore a gold wedding band. His voice carried a respectful but not overwhelming authority.

Long, the white officer, spoke sharply and

condescended to several inmates down the line. His uniform was ill-fitted and worn slovenly. Though big and tall, he appeared to be in worse shape than Broussard.

Count came to a close, and we returned to our cell for the night. I jumped back up onto my bunk and laid awake looking around the cell. Contrary to what you always see on television or in movies, modern prison cell doors are not iron bars but rather a solid door with a small window and slot for things to be handed in and out.

All of our clothes were stored, not in drawers, but in cubby holes. There was a small writing slat jutting out from the wall with a tiny plastic chair pushed up underneath it. In one corner sat the stainless steel toilet and sink. One single narrow window, barred of course, divided the outside wall.

My cellie had turned on a small color television, but it emitted no sound. For sound he tuned his small portable radio to a specific channel.

Barely audible from the top bunk, I watched the television, straining to hear the words. Nick was watching the continuing news coverage of Katrina's aftermath. The ticker tape scrolled across the bottom of the screen, but it was too small to read from that distance.

"You awake, fish?" He asked.

"Yeah."

"Was you on the coast when it hit?"

"I was." I kept my answers brief and to the point. I knew nothing about this man, and I didn't want to seem eager to make friends in here.

"Where about?" The questions from below continued.

"Bay Saint Louis, over in Mississippi," I replied.

"Family's in New Orleans. At least they was before the storm." I could hear the concern in his voice.

"They evacuate?"

"Need money for that. Food stamps don't pay for gas and motels, man." He quipped. "Sorry, just freaking out a bit. Ain't heard shit from em' yet."

"I'm sorry," and I truly was. During the storm I had felt isolated and trapped. I could only imagine what desperation he had felt while caged and unable to help those he loved when they needed him most.

"Your people make it through aight?"

"No."

He remained silent for a few minutes before changing the subject and bringing it to an abrupt halt. "Get some sleep. You got a long, boring day of nothing ahead of you tomorrow. No work assignments."

Saturday, June 3rd, 2006

About four thirty in the morning, I heard Nick moving around. I rolled over and rubbed the sleep from my eyes and asked him what he was doing.

"Morning chow, man. You coming?"

I nodded.

The food was less than gourmet, but as I was soon to discover, the breakfast fare was far better than any other meal of the day. Short of pleasure foods purchased from the commissary it was the best I was going to be eating for a long time to come.

I followed Nick to an empty table. Cons started gravitating towards our table- and Nick- as they entered the cafeteria. He was like a bright beam of light invading the darkness of this place. I am not saying that he was a happy-go-lucky ray of sunshine, but rather that he seemed to get respect from most of the other cons.

Quickly the table began to fill up. I was still tired, but hungry. I ate military style, head down, back straight, focused on my meal. I listened as those around me talked, but I had nothing to add to the conversation. Their words danced around me, about me even. "He looks like a pussy to me."

I ignored the remark and continued eating. Food came flying in my direction, landing in my plate, and I looked up for the first time. "Is you, boy? Is you a pussy?

I looked up at my instigator, a straight up thug nigga awaiting whatever rise he could get out of me. I sized him up. He looked to be barely twenty-one. Under each of his cold, crazy eyes was a tattooed tear. No need to guess what he was in for, murder.

The table was nearly silent, as everyone waited to see how I would react and what would pop off. I stood up, fork still in hand, holding his gaze.

"Oh shit, fish gonna bow up to you Tru! You gonna let that shit stand?" prodded one of his cronies.

"Shut up, Mano." He replied.

Finally, I spoke. "I realize it's been awhile, if ever, since you seen pussy, but rest assured it ain't me."

He leaned on the table, perplexed that I had stood up to him. Slick spoke up, "Er' one sit the fuck down. I'm still eatin. Ya'll start fightin and we all back to our cells without chow, an' if ya'll cause this fat boy to go hungry, we all gonna have some problems!"

Tru and I both eased back into our chairs, neither letting our guard down. Slick continued, shovelling food into his mouth as he spoke, "Inquiring minds obviously wanna know who the fuck you is, cellie. Out wit it, I wanna know who I stuck wit too."

Eyes were on me again. "I got a twenty year run. Name is AJ Jackson. Charges: Arson, Evading, Aiding, Breaking and Entering, those the ones I can remember."

Mouths stood slightly ajar, except for Slick. "Cool. At least I ain't stuck in here with some punk." He looked across the table and addressed the other cons, "Any of you motherfuckers got a problem wit my cellie?" Silence was the universal reply. "I didn't think so. Eat up or I'll do it for you."

A lot of adjustments were ahead of me, more than I could have ever imagined. Believe me, I had contemplated what prison might be like many times. When I was on the run I always had it in the back of my mind. When Shawn got arrested, I thought about it. In all my ponderings, I never once scratched the surface of what it truly was like behind prison walls.

Slick and I spent the rest of the afternoon talking.

I filled him in on the outside world as I had experienced it since he had been locked up. I told him about all my years on the run. I told him about riding out Katrina in Bay Saint Louis. Basically, I told him everything.

Before long he was sharing his background with me. He had been locked up for four years already after robbing a guy and nearly killing him, but robbery wasn't his original motive.

"Me an' my ole lady were leavin' the bar one night, right? An' this punk bitch decides he gonna try to lay his hands on Katie in the parkin' lot. He was drunk and pissed she had told him she had a man.

"I had been drinkin' since three that afternoon. Had two six's in me before gettin' to the bar, and when I get drunk I gonna fight. Especially when someone starts pawin' my girl. I was on him like stink on shit, dropping him to the blacktop. I wailed on him, rattling his head against the ground, clockin' him even after he was out. I kicked him a few times, grabbed his wallet as an afterthought, and the police arrived as we were getting' ready to pull out."

He grabbed a worn photo off the wall and handed it to me. It was his girl, Katie. She was a hot little number, no doubt, but street tough to be sure. She was a curvacous girl with blond hair and plenty of tats of her own. They were perfectly matched for each other.I nodded and handed it back.

"I never got to say it earlier, but thanks for chilling shit out at breakfast." I said.

"Ain't nothing but a thang man. Tru always looking to scrap. Fuckin' hothead, but he one of my boys. Way I look at it, fight gotta mean something for me to want to add time to my bid, an' that was just stupid earlier."

The rest of the day passed in relative silence, interrupted only by the occasional prisoner count. I laid on my bunk and tried to sleep away as much time as I could, but in the still moments I would find myself thinking about Charlotte, Christi, and my Lenny.

Was my life really so different from everyone else's on the fundamental level? Loss is inherently a part of life, for everyone. We are all dying, and the circles we travel in ensure that we will lose someone dear to us. Not only that, but over the course of a long life we can expect it to happen repeatedly.

For the first time perhaps, I saw myself as ordinary. I saw myself just as I was, with all of the media hype and controversy stripped away, and it filled me with serenity. I didn't need to be bigger than life anymore. I didn't have to be a shot-caller for anyone. I was left alone, more or less, with myself in this cell.

Many inmates cannot handle the introspection that confinement brings, but it did not bother me. I had years of experience dissecting the past and wondering a million what-if's. In that regard, prison was just another place to live my life. The regrets were going to always be with me in some form or fashion no matter where I was.

Don't get me wrong, the good times I kept in mind as well. I remembered fondly all the people I had helped, and I tried to envision the scales of justice in my mind and figure how evenly the good I had done balanced the pain and suffering I had brought others.

As the days passed my conclusion changed and changed again. A new memory would come to mind, long forgotten, and tip the balance once again for better or worse.

Days turned into weeks, and weeks in turn became months. I used my imposed sabbatical to better myself by studying books from the prison library, picking up my high school studies where I had left off so long ago. I also worked out with Slick, lifting weights quite often.

We became pretty good friends as time rolled on, and he kept me from more than one altercation. Though he was more learned in the ways of confinement, I knew that he respected me. He understood the motivations that had driven me to commit my crimes. He knew that I was doing my best to protect those that I loved in most cases. Very little of my acts against society were driven by actual greed or anger.

He also respected how long I had managed to elude authorities. Though I didn't really look the part, he always joked that inside I was a textbook psychopath. I knew he meant to say sociopath but lacked the proper terminology. What he lacked in education he most certainly made up for with his street smarts.

Slick showed me a million tricks for getting a hot meal in my cell and ways to sneak a smoke. He was innovative and taught me skills to make my stay there a little less constrictive.

Slick wasn't the only jailhouse friend that I made

at Pollack. Tru, as Trumaine Carter, Jr. was known, even ended up as one of them. He later explained to me that all new inmates are considered suspect when they first arrive, and I was no different. To the prison population in general, actions speak louder than words, and until you are given a chance to prove yourself through your actions or by keeping your mouth shut about the things you know others are doing, you will never be trusted or respected. Eventually I did gain his trust, and that was saying a lot since Tru had very little love for white people in general. There were only a handful of us crackers that he associated with on a regular basis.

He was a New Orleans native that had grown up in the Faubourg Tremé. He had to enlighten even me, one that had traveled and studied New Orleans, about the streets he was from. Tremé is the oldest black neighborhood in America, and it is known for its rich musical roots. (Years later, a cable channel would set a television show in the neighborhood only a few months post-Katrina.)

Armando O'Neal, or Mano as he was known on the block, was another of my friends. He was tough as nails and rivaled Slick as far as the number of tats he had, most of which was prison ink.

Born the son of an aspiring Irish prize fighter and and Puerto Rican mother in the Bronx, he learned from a young age how to fight. When it became apparent that his father's ambition was never going to be rewarded they moved to central Mississippi. He was fifteen at the time.

When I met him he was in his forties and had

spent most of his adult life in correctional facilities for violent crimes. Mano, Slick, and Tru were the three roughest in our circle, but not everyone I associated with was as prone to violence.

Wayne Maze, a scrawny kid in his early twenties, was Mano's cellie. Wayne was known on the block as Bunco because he had been a con man on the outside and had a surprising repertoire of scams for his age. He had worked block hustles, pigeon drops, and autograph scams.

It was an autograph scam that landed him in lockup. He had been circulating a bogus petition in order to collect signatures which he later used to forge checks. One of the doors he knocked on collecting signatures was a former mark that recognized him and reported him to the police. By that time he had already amassed three hundred signatures- and one count of fraud for each.

Vince Lockhart, nicknamed Hart, earned his ticket to Pollack by bookkeeping for an organized crime syndicate that opened up shop on the Mississippi coast after the legalization of dockside gambling in 1990.

He was expert at doctoring the books to hide profits that funded prostitution and drug running. Up until Katrina Hart had managed to stay in good with his connections on the outside enabling him to get just about anything you wanted, for the right price. He had been a man to know, but not one that you wanted to owe. Mano, Slick, and Tru were his enforcers and debt collectors and thus had enjoyed a few creature comforts here and there.

But life in Pollack, just as life on the outside, had been interrupted by the storm. People were still trying to pick up the pieces and reunite with family and friends. Hart's syndicate was every bit as scattered to the wind as traditional families, and for the first time in years he found himself without bargaining chips and owing others.

Agreements struck before the storm and paid for in advance, he found himself unable to make good on. Our crew was marked by this, and every day was a battle waiting to happen.

Though I came into the picture afterwards, I was guilty by association in the eyes of Hart's jilted customers. We all looked out for each other though. Prison is the kind of environment where gangs thrive, and although my intentions had been to do my time quietly, I still ended up right in the middle of things.

I spent each day carefully considering my actions and words, not wanting to exacerbate things further by saying or doing the wrong thing. As it turns out, despite my best attempts to avoid confrontations, I was on a collision course. I had failed to take into account the will of those always on the prowl for a fight.

CHAPTER FOURTEEN:
AN UNCOMFORTABLE STRETCH

The passage of time in prison is relative to the mindset of the prisoner. If you can find some focus for yourself the ride doesn't seem to drag on for quite so long, but if you can't, the hours become endless eternities and limbos in their own right.

By my second year, as I have said, I had found that working out and learning helped pass the time faster. I wrote when mood hit me, sometimes staying up through the night. My diversions made me feel more in control of my life. I tried to think of this as time given to me, rather than time taken from me.

Lord knows there is a list a mile long of things beyond your control in a penal institution, and it was about this point in my incarceration that I learned just how intertwined the lives of inmates really are.

Hart's enterprise was slowly returning as people came home to the area. He had worked out agreements with many of those that had been wronged, but not everyone. A few refused to have their deals renegotiated and still demanded they get their goods on their terms immediately.

I was in the yard on one of the rare occasions that I was not with my boys. I was lifting weights as was part of my routine. I had begun to bulk up for the first time in my life.

Slick was in the hole for his involvement in a lunchtime scuffle. Usually, we were each others' eyes when we were most vulnerable, but not on that particular day.

Midway through a set of reps, the bar was pushed down on my chest from both sides and a barrage of fists rained down on me. For at least ten minutes five guys worked me over, pinned down and helpless to fight back. The world went out of focus, and my body went numb. I could still feel the impact of the hits, but their stings were muted.

I woke up handcuffed to a bed in the infirmary. Long, Broussard, and one of the prison doctors were standing over me. "How you feeling?" asked the doctor.

"Like I was hit by a fucking train. What the hell happened?"

"We were hoping you could tell us," Officer Long said snidely. He seemed to hold a special contempt for me, above and beyond what he harbored against the other inmates. In this respect, he reminded me of Houston Fields and his disdain for JP.

"I was working out, and someone jumped me. That's all I know." It wasn't the total truth. I knew that there were multiple attackers. I caught enough of a look at one of them to recognize his face, Bennie Lusk. Bennie was, not surprisingly, one of Hart's pissed off former customers.

"I think you know exactly why they came for you, Jackson." Long prodded.

"Long…" Broussard attempted to calm the obviously worked up guard.

"Well, I don't. Sorry." I replied.

Long launched into another attempt to get me to talk. "What was it? Drug deal gone bad?"

"Officer Long please wait outside," requested Broussard. Hesitantly, Long left the room, and Broussard came closer and spoke in a softer tone.

"Son, I know who you are. Everyone knows. It's beyond me why they chose to put you into Gen Pop and not Ad Seg. If you help me out with this maybe I can make some calls and get you moved where you can serve out your time in safety. If you choose to be uncooperative they will add time to your bid. So you got anything to tell me?"

Broussard was a straight shooter, even with cons, but I knew he didn't have the pull to move me out of general population even if I did rat out Hart's business endeavors. That wasn't going to happen anyways, so I sat definitely silent.

"Alright, Jackson, have it your way." With that he was gone, remanding me in the care of the doctor. My vitals were checked and pain medication was administered. It was several days before I was released back into Gen Pop, still severely bruised.

It was a close call. I was surprised they hadn't tried to stick me. Death was common at Pollack. It was a rough place. A guy had been killed by another inmate just two weeks prior.

When I returned to the block, I found Slick out of the hole. When Broussard had left, Slick commented on my condition, "This is fucked up, bro! Who da fuck did this?"

He was outraged. He put his fist to the wall.

"Lusk and some of his boys paid me a visit in the yard. Guess they still upset with Hart's business ethics." I replied.

"Guards get you to talk?"

I gave him a disappointed look. "Are you serious? I thought you knew by now that I ain't no fucking rat!"

"I do, but I been wrong before. When they start talkin' bout adding time to your bid lips get real loose sometimes." Slick stood looking at me and extended his hand. I shook it.

The next day in the yard Hart tried to slide me a pack of smokes. It was his way of saying thanks for not blowing the whistle on his operation. I told him to keep them and that while I appreciated the gesture; the guards were watching me closer.

And it was the truth. At every turn the guards, especially Long, seemed to be keeping tabs on me. To allow Hart to put him self at risk by passing contraband would have made me just as culpable for what would happen to him as if I had ratted.

I told him, "If you wanna make it up to me just keep me out of the fucking infirmary in the future." He nodded. "And no retaliation either. Just let it ride."

I was trying to stave off a war- the back and forth attacks that would inevitably follow would do nothing to get me released any sooner. That was all I cared about, getting back to my Lenny. I didn't care a bit about prison pride, but I suppose I should have. To not take vengeance upon your enemies in prison for jumping you make you look like a punk.

Time was added to my bid, a full year to be exact. In one day's time, the whole last year that I had worked so hard to keep my nose clean and do quiet time was erased. It dawned on me that I might be there a very, very long time passed my original scheduled release date.

Still I kept my silence. It was a virtue that commanded respect, but honestly I didn't have much of a choice. To squawk to officials would be suicide, and that wasn't on my planned agenda either.

I would simply have to try harder to stay clear of the drama. I had to find my resolve to get out of Pollack as soon as possible.

CHAPTER FIFTEEN: CORRESPONDENCE

Awhile back, there had been a television special regarding my capture and incarceration. The crew was not allowed to interview me, and I have not had a chance to view the program. The only reason I know of the show's existence at all is because of the dramatic increase in the amount of "fan" mail I began receiving immediately following its air date.

Being the somewhat self-absorbed guy I am, I read every last letter sent to me. I suppose even if I wasn't as obsessed with what the world thought of me as I was I would have read them anyways out of sheer boredom. Hell, David Bowie started every day reading all the newspaper clippings about himself, so why not me?

I would like to say that I replied to all of the letters that I got, but I didn't. I did reply to most of them. Some seemed like they were a bit unstable, but most were normal kids or people that had been kids when we were in our heyday. Many sent me books of stamps hoping it would increase their chances of getting a reply, and it did.

One girl in particular wrote often, and we became penpals. Her name was Amanda Silver, a fitting name since she had both a heart of gold and wrote the most precious letters. Her first read as follows:

Dear AJ,

My name is Amanda. I don't know where to begin. This is the first time I have written a letter to someone in jail. I graduated this year from high school in Sikeston, Missouri. Only twenty miles and several years difference and we would have been neighbors.

I used to daydream that I was on that bus the day yall left Dexter, and that I got to travel around and see the country with you. I guess over the years I've kinda developed a bit of a crush on you. Don't laugh, I know it is silly, but it is true.

I just wanted to write and get to know you better. I'll leave it at that and see if I get a reply before writing more.

Hoping to Hear from You,

Amanda xoxox

We exchanged many letters over the course of the next year of my incarceration, but I felt that I was not a very good influence on this young woman with her whole life ahead of her. One day, something just clicked, and I stopped replying to her letters. I still read them for the next month or so, but eventually I felt so lousy for not replying that I stopped doing that even.

There were others that wrote. Not all were women, in fact it was about fifty-fifty ratio across the sexes. Not all were adoring fans either. There was a low percentage of hate mail that I received as well. Rarely did I respond to any of these unless something they had wrote really compelled me to either explain myself or fire right back at them.

One of these hate letters in particular I remember. A mother in Salt Lake City claimed I was solely responsible for her son's juvenile delinquent tendencies. I refused to let that letter go unanswered. I told her bluntly that if she spent more time with her child, bothered to teach him the values that she should have been raised with, and cared enough to monitor his pop culture in-take, his path probably could have been altered before it had gotten to the point he was at.

Parents who blame society and mass media for everything that ails their family really piss me off. Do commercials really brainwash people into thinking they can't live without certain products or services? Of course! That is their sole mission, but guess what, when

I was growing up, my seniors had known the secret. You turn the damn volume down or go take a piss during the commercial and don't subject yourself to it over and over! Anyways, I digress.

I also received letters from Ben and Mrs. Foxworth, but it was always a chore finding them in the morass of incoming correspondence.

Ben and I wrote back and forth the entire time I was incarcerated at Pollack. I told him about the life Charlotte and I had shared. I told him about Katrina and many of the things I have already shared in this book. He told me about his latest successes with his publishings and kept my commissary account full so that I could purchase the things I needed.

Once, I thanked him for it, and his reply had been that it was money earned from his comic book adaptation of the adventures of the Brat Pack. In short, he was telling me that it was my money anyways.

Ben wrote to inform me that Charlotte's remains had been found. He flew to Bay Saint Louis to identify the body. He let me know that he had bought her a crypt in New Orleans with a beautiful statue that would forever look over her remains. She was home.

Mrs. Foxworth wrote monthly at best but always sent recent photos of Lenny. When photos weren't included, there was always something else whether it was something Lenny had colored for me or copies of his report card. In a way, these were the letters that I dreaded the most.

Letters from strangers were entertaining, but I did not, in most cases long for them. Letters from those I loved and could not be with hurt. It was wonderful to know that Lenny was doing great in school and had a fantastic life, but the bittersweet truth was I was always reminded just what I had lost out on.

So much time still would have to pass before I was able to hug him again, and by that time he would be nearly grown. The heartaches and growing pains of adolescence, he would suffer without daddy around to give face-to-face advice or comfort him.

Going into my fourth year of incarceration (2010) Mrs. Foxworth started allowing Lenny to write to me directly. Again, I both looked forward to and dreaded his letters.

We lived in parallel universes, each with knowledge of the other's existence yet equally unable to bridge the gap to cross over. I tried to make him understand that I loved him and hoped that his love for me had not diminished over the years. We had the best relationship that we could under the circumstances.

Holidays were extremely difficult at Pollack as they were milestones of lost time and memories. I called Lenny as often as I could on holidays so that he would always know his father was thinking about him.

He was fourteen by then and smart as a tack. He was perfection to me. Nothing could lift my spirits like hearing his voice. Often I had to cut the calls short because I could feel the tears coming on as my emotions would start to get the better of me.

Letters and a handful of phone calls was my connection to the world passing me by outside the walls of Pollack. Sometimes it was easiest to forget there even was another world out there and focus on my immediate needs inside the cell.

I rarely paid any attention to the television, choosing instead to spend my time reading or writing. The act of creating something new always engaged me and appealed to me more than passively watching the slow march of time outside.

CHAPTER SIXTEEN:
TENSIONS RISE

You could have cut it with a shiv; the tension in the air. Only three months into 2010 and there had been four inmate killed by Pollack guards' use of excessive force. Broussard had been gone for about six months at the time. Long was still there and had been involved in two of the four murders.

Guards and inmates alike seemed to be watching over their shoulders constantly. The inmates were getting restless and felt helpless to protect themselves from the guards, and that helplessness they redirected to their fellow cons. Fights broke out almost daily.

Rumor had it that so many people had been sent to the hole that they had run out of room.

It was times like these when I was comforted to have made the friends that I had in Pollack. I was determined that I would walk out those doors in one piece when my time was up, and I wanted the same for those that helped make that possible for me. There was a price to pay, though.

Wednesday, March 10th 2010

That week there were countless inmates that sustained injuries serious enough to send them to the infirmary. The fights were getting bigger, with more inmates participating in them, and on this day we found ourselves involved.

Bunco was stuck with a shiv while returning to the block from yard time. Tru and I happened to be with him and promptly began kicking and punching his attacker. It became a madhouse as other inmates began attacking us or each other. Guards were dispatched in full riot gear. Canisters of tear gas were launched up on our tier. I began to cough and my eyes watered and burned.

Still, the fighting did not subside. Fists were flung with further abandon, blindly hoping to hit anyone. Inmates turned on the guards and rushed them en masse, forcing them to retreat outside of the block.

Everyone knew this was coming. It was an inevitable forgone conclusion. Bunco and I had been counting on it and waiting patiently for it to happen, but we never expected to be in the middle of its initiation. Perhaps I should explain.

Bunco and I had become very good friends and had been working on a prison break that would free both of us, as well as Slick, Tru, and Hart. We planned to walk right out the front door free and unfettered men. Bunco was the key to this stroke of brilliance, or rather his uncanny ability to forge documents was.

Hart managed to procure the blank release forms. Bunco had worked his magic on the forms choosing random release dates. Slick was the carrier, tasked with hiding and carrying our papers on his person. From that point all we could do was wait for the riot that would no doubt occur soon.

Today happened to be that day. In the confusion Slick was able to grab the keys from Long who was being beaten mercilessly and sneak over to the administrative wing and deliver the documents into each of our files. He barely made it back before the lockdown had occurred.

By the time the guards reclaimed the block, Bunco had bled out. We retreated into our cells, hoping to avoid as little wrath as possible from the approaching victors. Slick assured me that he had found everyone's files without issue. We were golden. All that remained was to keep our noses clean until our release dates.

Tuesday, April 13th, 2010

Hart's date had finally arrived, and we would finally know if our rouse was going to work. We all watched with anticipation to see if he would make it out or not. We tried to conceal our excitement as the time drew nearer, but damn it was hard. If this worked, we would soon be following him right out the front doors and back to our real lives.

We were scared to get our hopes up, but how could we not? Hope and time was all we had, and what more fertile ground for dreams does anyone need than that?

I knew I had my future planned out. When I got out I was leaving this country once and for all. I knew I would write of our escape eventually and the pieces would be put together, but by that time Lenny and I would be out of reach. Even if I never wrote of it, surely a security tape somewhere had to have caught Slick planted the documents in our files, so I might as well write about it and send a nice *fuck you* to Pollack.

I was scared to tell the others that I planned to write of our prison break, so I kept it to myself. These were cons that would do anything to keep their impending liberty intact. I wanted to tell them, invite them to leave the country and start a new life with me, but I could not risk their resistance.

Finally the wait was over; we would at last have our answer. Hart emerged from his cell, trying to contain his smile, dressed in his civilian clothes. Guards escorted him out none the wiser.

In the yard that afternoon we all celebrated silently and remembered our brother, Bunco, who had made it all possible. I kept waiting for everyone to speak in hushed tones of what their plans for the outside were, but no one did. They were afraid of jinxing it. To talk about it is to invite disaster.

I was pleased that it was Hart who was first out. His business was dead as far as our click was concerned. We wanted only to keep ourselves out of trouble and get the hell out of Pollack. We no longer had to worry that his activities would be discovered. It was a relief.

Tru followed him to freedom two weeks later. Slick and I were left to ride out our time with our crew whittled down to only the two of us. As cellies at least we had each other for company until Slick's date.

He could not wait, but I was a bit nervous being the last out. I would have one month longer to wait once he vacated our cell. In that time there would be no one to watch my back. Though I had bulked up in prison, I was still far from intimidating.

Anyone that has ever been to prison and released knows how scared you get right before it happens. You start worrying that something will mess it up, like a fight or someone planting contraband on you to get you in trouble or what not. It doesn't take much for it to all fall to shit. All the enemies you have made along the way can't wait to derail the process for you.

Some inmates request Ad Seg for their last stretch because they get worried they will fuck it up for themselves. Some are terrified about reentering society, having been under lock and key for so long. Not me. June 22nd could not come soon enough. I was fully ready to be emancipated.

CHAPTER SEVENTEEN:
THE LAST STRETCH

I woke up early on Friday, May 21st. It was Slick's release date. I was happy for him that he was going to once again be holding his girl Katie in his arms. I was happy he would be reunited with what was left of his family. Still, I was sad that I was losing him.

He had become my best friend, my roommate over the past four years. In my mind I wondered if the walls of Pollack would crumble without ole Slick Goode holding them up. If, perchance, they did, should I run away early, or wait out my remaining days with just a little more sunlight in my cell?

I knew the walls wouldn't crumble, but he had become central to keeping the peace on our block. The few times he couldn't keep the peace, he brought down wrath that made people think twice about questioning him the next time.

I wondered how he would adapt back into life on the outside. I wondered if Katie had waited on him. Judging from her letters she loved him very deeply, but words can be twisted and faked. I hoped for his sake that she appreciated having him back with her. After all, it was because of her that he had ended up here in the first place.

I wondered if he would fly right, or if he would cling to the ways of the streets and cells. No matter what the future held for him, I knew Nick "Slick" Goode was a survivor just like me.

"Man, I'm gonna miss the hell outta you boy!" He said as he prepared to make his walk out. I went to shake his hand, but he wasn't having it. Today was his day, and by God, he wanted a hug. I stood, staring at him, like *get the fuck out of here*, but alas succumbed.

"See man, ain't life a little better with a lil' bromance?" He smiled, which made me laugh. "Just so long as that's all the bro-mance you get into in here." As he walked out of the cell he looked back one last time and left me with these words, "Don't worry. You'll be out in no time, playa. Holla at your boy if you get a chance."

The door closed. It was hard to believe he was gone and not simply riding out a stint in the hole. The quiet for the first time really bothered me. Even in prison, I had managed to find myself with friends. I started to ponder my uncanny ability to lose everything and everyone.

I wasn't sad in the traditional sense. Our plan had worked. We were all going to be free. They just had a head start getting back to their lives. Without any better ideas what to do next I took a nap.

When I awoke a few hours later I set about making preparations for my release, scheduled for June 22nd. I wrote Ben and told him the good news. I didn't write Lenny though. I was afraid to get his hopes up and have something go wrong. As best as I could, that was always the one thing I tried to avoid doing, disappointing my child.

I rarely left my cell, figuring that the less I did, the better my chances of avoiding altercations were. Much of this time I spent writing. I wrote a few short stories and dozens of poems. Perhaps I will include them in this volume.

One story, which I have yet to write, continues to nag at me. I woke one morning from a dream with the seeds of this particular story sown so deeply it bypassed the almost instant onset of amnesia that comes with waking.

The dream was about a husband, wife and their six year old daughter and what happened to them when they moved to a very odd town. It played in my mind as a cross between *Children of the Corn* and *The Stepford Wives*. The town seemed to have its own new age religion. The pastor of the local church seemed to take a peculiar interest in the child.

This interest came from an ability the child seemed to possess to bring a free will to those the pastor had entranced, making them lose their faith in him and his teachings. With nothing more than her innocent questioning of why, she could topple his budding empire.

Perhaps, one day I will write that one, but I was confident that I would not lose the imagery of the dream to time so I decided to wait.

There were other stories that I had in various stages of completion, mostly in the horror genre, that I had vowed to finish before undertaking new endeavors. These were part of a collection I had named *Haunted Ears* and were written in the form of an anthology a la *Tales from the Crypt*.

To give you a sense of how slowly those last days drug by for me, I am going to include a few of those short stories from *Haunted Ears* before concluding my account. You will notice reoccurring themes within the stories, no doubt dredged up from childhood memories regarding my real parents. Every writer does this, I feel, to some extent.

CHAPTER EIGHTEEN:
HAUNTED EARS:
THE TORMENTED STEPHEN BRACKEN

The Dead should simply shut up! I can stand their tormented cries and confessions no longer. I am what remains of Stephen Bracken, the once-great horror novelist. You haven't read anything of mine lately? Oh, that is because I have sat here in this sanitarium for years barely able to hear the living for the never-ending clamor of the not-so-dearly-departed. Surely someone somewhere found them dear, but not me. To hell with them, and to hell with me also.

I used to believe my condition was a gift, and indeed, two of my best-selling novels, *Behind Cold Eyes* and *Blessed Retribution*, were derived from words once whispered from beyond someone's grave. Finally, there came a day when I could no longer shut out the voices, and my gift mutated into a curse.

Ghostly whispers in the dark of night disturb the serenity of my sleep. When I finally do manage to muster a peaceful dream I find it abruptly ruined by the laughs and screams of the other lunatics. It makes me wonder how crazy they are and how sane our keepers are. I don't really care that much though. After all, soon I will be leaving their ranks. No, I am not getting out. I rant and rock in my seat far too often to pass for normal, whatever that is. That is why I have been deposited here for the rest of my natural born life by my dear brother, Brent Bracken. Being the good big brother he is, he has been kind enough to watch over my fortune for me.

His visits are growing more infrequent. I know the reason why. Ask and he denies it, but he is afflicted the same as me, only to a lesser degree. He has always caught the distant whispers of souls too weak to shout. I have seen him cock his head in response. The whisperers are the easy ones to ignore. It started that way for me as well, and as the years passed the living world slowly grew silent and the dead found fuller voices with which to heap anguish on me.

As I was saying, soon I shall end my life and rush the very threshold of Heaven and Hell. Hearing spirits as I do, I don't really have to have faith in a hereafter; I know it exists! I doubt that Heaven will have me, but

Hell could not possibly be worse than drawing these burdened breaths. Before I make this final voyage I have one last task to complete. I must pass along the tales told to me by those rotting elsewhere who have not the breath to tell others directly. I must put them to paper as they have hounded me to do so that I might find peace in death.

Those I leave behind will not mourn me. Have they not already abandoned me? My friends stopped visiting long ago. Oh I'm sure they will hover over the box my mortal remains get stuffed in, but inside of them joyful hearts will beat. Their tears will reek of happiness. What a social event it will be for the literary types!

Brent is my last living blood relative. Our parents passed on last year, just shortly after my twenty-seventh birthday, which went uncelebrated. A car crash claimed both of their lives. The very hour of their passing brought their voices to my ears. I focused in on their voices and listened, tuning out all others. That night did they wish to send their undying love to their son? No, they felt it important to let me know once more what a disappointment I had been to the family, even before my breakdown. "You'll never be more than a two-bit hack, Stephen!" my father hissed.

Mom added, "Writing filth isn't art. It's pornography!"

I was born to lose my hearing, my fortune, my freedom, and my family. Soon I will die to triumph though. Let me now bare for you the souls of others while I still have the tongue to tell what my haunted ears have heard.

I shall begin with the story of Corey Kline. It was his story that inspired me to indulge myself in the ultimate act of self-absorption: Suicide.

CHAPTER NINETEEN:
HAUNTED EARS:
COREY KLINE JUMP SOME OTHER TIME

After ten years of marriage to both Mary and the firm I found myself divorced and downsized. I put the cardboard box containing the contents of my desk drawers in the trunk of the Mustang. On the drive home, I shut out the world. All I could think about was getting home to Mary. No matter what happened it had always been us against the world. Why should today be any different?

She was diddling someone else, most likely, my friend Paul, the butcher. His meat was much more to her liking than my own I guess. She had other reasons too. We had been going to a marriage counselor for several months. As things went downhill at work, I was able to get it up less and less. We were both frustrated with the situation, and I guess she just got tired of trying to fix it.

Mary hadn't taken everything. No, she left our greedy brats for me to raise. Amber was seven, and Arnold was nine at the time. They were both rotten and ungrateful. Nothing was ever good enough for them. Some days I had worked late just so I wouldn't have to be around them as long at night. Now I didn't even have an office for escape.

Mom had just recently passed away. My father was in a nursing home. I can honestly say that I did not have one single thing going for me. Is it any wonder that I was ready to fling myself from my office building?

I was standing on the edge, ready to let myself freefall backwards. The wind was blowing hard. I was eager to feel the winds caress my body as I descended. I closed my eyes and leaned back. A hand snatched at my shirt. Was I falling yet? No.

Tom Groom, our former – unsuccessful - marriage counselor, had a hold of me. The prick was built like Conan. "Let go, Tom, damn it!" I tried to break loose and continue my death dive, but nothing was going to slip from his kung-fu grip. He shook his head and launched me back over onto the roof. I landed hard. "What the hell are you doing here?"

"Mary called. She told me you was acting strange the last time you two talked."

"Strange, huh? I am ready to flush away this shit heap of a life!" I looked up.

"Corey, I know you and Mary have been going through some rough times, but it can't be that bad," he said. At this I could not help but laugh.

I stood up and approached him. "Rough times? Did you know that Mary's been fucking my best friend? That's a bit more than a rough time in my book." I counted my woes on my fingers for him. "I got canned earlier. Now I have to find another way to provide for the two ungrateful brats that bitch left with me. My Dad is getting worse by the day. I have nothing!"

He said nothing for a moment. "Look what are you trying to do here? You want to escape all these problems. Fine! Go ahead and do it, but you don't have to kill yourself. It is much too extreme of a solution for these temporary problems."

I shrugged. "I am not going to some loony bin."

He quieted me. "I didn't say you should. You aren't crazy. We both know that. You just need to get away. You are having trouble adjusting to several significant changes in your living situation." I glared at him, not quite trusting him. "Will you do me a favor?"

"What?"

"Make me a deal. Take off and just vanish for six months. Cut ties with everyone."

"Everyone?" I asked.

"Everyone, damn it. Reevaluate all your relationships, and get rid of the clutter in your life. Any person or thing in your life that troubles you, just remove it from your life."

"It makes sense, but it isn't a deal. A deal involves a compromise. Are you saying that if I do as you ask and in six months I still want to die, you will leave me to it?" He nodded, and I thought it over. Did I want to do this? Could I do it? Hell, if I could fling myself off a building why couldn't I do this? What would it mean? It would mean leaving behind everything familiar and starting from scratch. It would mean paying no bills, keeping no appointments, and worrying about no one except myself. Complete and total freedom prescribed by my therapist. Yes, I could do this.

"Many would frown on me for even suggesting such a radical idea, but I am not about to lose one of my patients." He smiled. "You said your job let you go earlier. They must have given you a handsome severance check, right?" I nodded.

"Okay, Tom. It's a deal, but I am not paying for this session."

I went home and told the kids to get ready to go to the movies. I packed my things while they got ready. They had no idea as they got into the car that the trunk was filled with what belongings I valued enough to take with me. I gave them money for their tickets, and then after they hounded me for a few minutes I gave them more for their concessions. I left them there unsuspecting. On my way out of Nashville I phoned Mary's parents and told them to pick the kids up from a movie and keep them for a few days.

I drove around aimlessly for several hours. Now I had the complete freedom I had always dreamed of attaining, but I had no idea what to do with it. I parked beside a small man-made lake in Dickson, Tennessee, and I sat there in the car looking at my reflection in the mirror. There I was, and how pathetic I felt. I was fast approaching forty, balding, and the heaviest I had ever been, which was two hundred pounds.

I finally made myself leave the warm car, intending to walk once around the lake. Winter was coming on fast making the night air cold. Shuffling along, I looked at my feet. Duck shit littered the road and grass alike. I plunged my hands deep in the pockets of my leather jacket and began a walk of introspection. Looking out at the lake made me think of summers past, spent on my grandparents' farm outside of Dexter, Missouri. They had a small pond on their property.

I had fond recollections of those times. I remember swimming and fishing in that pond. Some times I would simply row the boat out to the middle and fall asleep looking up at the puffy clouds. Grandpa didn't mind if I took the boat out. He would just wave at me on his way through to throw trash into a ravine at the back of his property. He used it as his own private dump. I wasn't allowed back there, but it didn't matter because there were so many other things to do on the farm.

A small pigsty that was no longer in use had been converted into a basketball court. I had miles and miles of woods to hike any time I wanted. My dad kept his little dune buggy on the farm so I could take it up to the field and take laps when I wanted to do so. I also got to help the transients with the farm work.

Grandpa called them drifters and hobos and seemed to hold them in low esteem. Still, he always found work for them, fed them, and sent them on their ways. He was set in his ways, but he was a good man.

A cold breeze brought me out of my memories, and I struggled to remember the last time that I had been back to the property. When you are working it gets hard to get away and do the things you want. Grandma and grandpa had died long ago. I didn't even know if the old house was still standing, and with nothing holding me back, I went to find out.

I arrived near midnight. The full moon shone brightly overhead. Because the gravel road was so washed out, I parked at the base of the giant hill on which the house sat. Flashlight in hand, I climbed toward the dilapidated house. The intervening twenty some-odd years had not been kind to the structure.

The white paint was flaking. Trash littered the porch where the swing hung from one side only. The front door was locked for what good it did being that one of the glasses in it was broken out. I hesitated at the threshold, and then entered into the living room.

It was as cold inside as it was outside. I could tell the wood stove had not been used in ages. I let the beam of my flashlight scan the room. The little television stand held a small broken television hiding under the same thick layer of dust that covered everything here. The old grandfather clock still stood like a sentry in the corner, by the doors to the bedrooms, but wore the wrong time. I tried, without any luck, to turn on the overhead light and then, in turn, the lamp at the end of the musty old couch. The curtains were in tatters and swaying in the breeze brought by more broken windows behind the couch.

I walked into the kitchen. The floor had sunken in on one side. From the fridge, I assumed, came the reeking stench of spoiled food. Its only purpose now was to hold the odds and ends my grandmother always kept out of my reach on top of it.

I spent the next fifteen minutes looking over the rest of the house. The experience did nothing to elevate my spirits. The closure of knowing what had become of this Mecca of fond memories only heaped more melancholy on me. The longer I thought about it, though, I understood this was where I needed to be now.

It seemed that no one would bother me here. I would have the quiet to ponder my relationships as the good Dr. Groom had suggested. Perhaps I could leave the place in a better state than I found it. Yes, I would stay.

I carefully drove the Mustang on up closer to the house. No need to advertise I was squatting illegally. After building a fire in the wood stove to warm my new quarters, I toted my belongings inside. I shook the dust off an old cover and laid it in the floor a short distance from the stove. A bundle of clothes sufficed for a pillow, and soon the warmth left me drowsy.

I slept soundly through the night, but a dream caused me to wake with a start. In the dream I could see myself asleep on the floor. The ceiling tiles overhead were slowly turning red until the blood that was saturating them finally brought them down on me. They pelted me transferring their bloody coating to my skin. As I sat up in horror in my dream I awoke doing the same. Though I was not bloody as I had been in the dream, I felt dirty and diseased. I had to get cleaned up before anything else.

There was no running water much less hot water, so I grabbed a change of clothes and walked back to the pond to clean up as best I could. It was cold enough that I could see my morning breath so I knew it wasn't going to be a pleasant experience getting into the water. I shucked my clothes off and laid them on the old aluminum boat. I quickly jumped in not wanting to prolong this ordeal. My body was having a hard time figuring out if it was freezing or scalding as I quickly lathered up the soap in hand and cleaned up. I rushed to the bank to get back to my clothes, and I tripped on something in the water. I fell face first.

I dried off and dressed as quickly as I could and made my way back down to the house. The fire had all but gone out, but still it was warmer than outside. I lay back down for a minute, basking in the relative heat and listening to my stomach groan its displeasure with being neglected. The ceiling tiles were all still in their proper place and without a trace of blood to be found anywhere.

I pulled the door closed behind me and went into town to get something to eat from the deli of Dexter's lone grocery store. Soon my belly was full once again. Biscuits and gravy and a cup of coffee; nothing special. I sat long thinking back on my younger years spent on my grandparents' farm. I missed the way things were back then, simpler. I missed my innocence. So many years had got behind me, ones filled with so many transgressions and shameful deeds. I knew I could never regain the precious commodity lost to time.

Further, I wasn't sure where I was going in life. I mean just yesterday I stood teetering over the edge of building ledge ready to cash in the chips. What was the point of fixing up my grandparents' old farmhouse? The point was to simply stay busy and not sit around counting the ways my life was shit.

I purchased a few things while I was at the store and returned home- if you want to call it that. I put the goods inside and went back outside. I found an old ax and put it to use cutting firewood. God bless the inventor of the chainsaw. How I wished grandpa hadn't been so cheap as to not own one!

I went inside to rest after I had ranked enough wood on the porch to last a day or two. It was late afternoon by this time. I emptied my pockets onto the table and noticed something was missing. My keys were nowhere to be found. No need to get worked up about it, I wasn't going anywhere tonight. I was exhausted and filthy from working hard all day. I still had things to do before dark. I'd look for them later. I stoked up the fire and fed it a hefty log, emptied the ashes from underneath, and set about to cover the breezeways created by missing windows in the house.

"Almost time to relax," I said aloud to myself as I placed a pot on top of the stove and filled it with the better part of a gallon of bottled water. Soon I was washing up in relative style with a rag and warm water.

As the twilight eased into night, I lit some candles and broke out my new flashlight. The front room was getting nice and warm, and I longed for a nice cup of sassafras tea. My grandpa and I used to dig up saplings and use their roots to make it years ago. Nothing was better on a cold day than a warm cup of tea. For those of you that do no know, the sassafras root is the natural flavoring put into root beer. It is also what the Indians used for aspirin and blood thinning. In large enough doses one can get rather light-headed and euphoric. Maybe I'd go and dig me up a sapling tomorrow, right after I solved the enigma of the missing keys. I could use a bit of euphoria.

In the meantime, I figured why not explore. Flashlight in hand, I walked to my grandparents' old bedroom. Everything they had owned, from the rocking chair that sat in the corner to grandpa's various shotguns and rifles, was still in place. Did someone in the family still own the land? Why had they not boxed up or sold off all the valuable heirlooms that remained?

The closet still held clothes, or I should say what was left of them. A rat left its tracks in the dusty film covering the bed. I walked on through the door adjoining their room to the one that I had used while staying with them. I would have to answer nature's call soon, but first I wanted a quick peek. The floor had sunk in on one side just like the kitchen had. I let my eyes follow my flashlight's beam. I walked to the table directly in front of me. The old lamp that had been my night-light remained. The window behind the table swayed.

I had not yet covered the windows in the other rooms. I pulled the curtains apart to see what was in store for me when I did get to this one. Tap. A Latino man stood eye to eye with me. He was missing an arm, and his good arm was coved in blood also. He laid his bloody palm flat on the window, and his blood streaked down the windowpane. I fell back to the floor, struggling to recover my flashlight. I shined it once again to the window to find the man gone, but the bloody trail of his hand on the window remained.

I eased my way back out of the room. My eyes never left the window the whole time. I snatched up one of the shotguns from grandpa's room and checked to see if it was loaded. Grandpa had always kept his guns loaded so I wasn't surprised to find it ready to go.

I had two choices: go out and try to find out who my mystery company was or wait until he decided he wanted to come to me. Better the next meeting is on my terms and at a time of my choosing I figured. I opened the front door and let the barrel of the gun lead the way into the country darkness.

The light of the heavens aided my battery-powered beam in illuminating my way around the back of the house. My steps were slow and sure and as quiet as I could make them. The shotgun was loaded and cocked, but I feared it would not fire if it came to that. I said a silent prayer as I rounded the corner quickly looking for the outsider. I stood alone with my gun. I walked to the window and found it without the bloody handprint.

I know what I saw. I knew even then I had not imagined the looker in the window, but I had no clue what in the hell was happening. I went back inside cautiously and moved the television in front of the door to slow any would-be intruder. My bladder was ready to explode. Shotgun still in hand I walked down the hall passed grandpa's old wardrobe to the bathroom.

I sat the gun against the sink and relieved myself. I peered out the bathroom window fearing a repeat of earlier. No eyes looking back at me, just the empty darkness. I picked up the gallon of water by my feet and dumped enough in the toilet to make it flush.

I had barely passed the wardrobe when I heard a loud, deep scream. I turned to face whatever had made the noise but saw nothing. I leaned closer to the wardrobe, the seeming source, trying to see what could possibly be between the minute space between it and the wall. The quarters were too close to pull the shotgun out and aim, so I was on my own this time. The voice bellowed out again.

I mustered my courage and sat the gun down. While one hand shined the flashlight the other hand reached for the wardrobe's edge. I hoped to move it out to get a better look. A hand, dark as midnight, followed by an arm grabbed my hand. Blood covered it and caused it to have to readjust its grip on me over and over, but it was strong.

Who could be slim enough to stand in such a small area? Pain rushed over me as it began to clamp down harder on my hand. It moaned, and I heard the bones in my hand popping. I strained to reach the shotgun, and when I finally reached it, I wasted no time pulling the trigger. No need to aim. I felt some of the buckshot scatter hitting both my arm and that of my attacker. It recoiled and went back behind the wardrobe.

I wasn't about to stay in the house and my keys were nowhere in sight. I pulled on the front door, knocking the television out of the way. I realized just how much it would have helped if someone were trying to get in through the front door. Out in the cold of night with only my gun and flashlight for the second time tonight, I went to the only place I would feel secure.

I flipped the old boat over and grabbed the oars. I tossed the shotgun aboard and shoved off from the pond's bank. All I had to do was stay in the middle of the pond until daylight. I could find my keys when the sun came up and make my retreat in haste.

My arm was bleeding still, but my wounds were not life threatening. I was more worried about the broken bones in my hand. I tossed the small anchor overboard and laid back. The boat's aluminum body was cold, but it felt good. So did the security I felt having serene waters to protect me. Any intruders would have a hard time getting to me without alerting me to their comings.

The more I lay there and contemplated the day's strange occurrences the less sense they made. Who was the man in the window? Why did he look familiar? How could anyone have fit behind the wardrobe? As I tried to wrap my mind around these questions, I found an uneasy, uncomfortable sleep.

I awoke as the first warm colors were brightening the horizon. The boat was rocking though the surrounding waters were halcyon. Dare I look over the edge? No. I reached instead for the double barrel shotgun and its lone loaded barrel. Was it a snake or a turtle? Was it something more sinister? I didn't care to find out. If it poked its head out of the water it was going to be unhappy. That was all I knew.

I nervously watched the boat's perimeter and my own back. Then I saw it. A child's hand grasp at the side of the boat. Both hands latched on, and it pulled itself up into the boat. The kid wasn't very old, maybe a year at most. He had been dead for longer than that. His skin was slimy and bloated and was missing its head. Somehow blood was still gushing from the neck along with puss.

I knew what would happen if I fired on this miniscule phantom inside the boat. I would blast holes into it and sink my vessel. I didn't care though. I had to put this thing out of its misery. It was crawling right for me, clawing at the boat's bottom. I fired the gun, obliterating it and puncturing the boat's thin aluminum skin. My ears were ringing and failed to process vital auditory data that I could have used.

More hands were latching on to the sinking boat's sides. I was overrun with the bodies of other children in various stages of decay. They all had one thing in common, no head. They were adding more weight by the second, sinking the boat faster. I abandoned my besieged boat and swam for the bank.

I felt hands grabbing at me the whole way. Soaked and scared I ran back towards the house. As much as I didn't want to venture back inside the house, I had to find my keys and get the hell out of there.

The door was still standing open, as I had left it. I crossed the threshold and I realized where the keys were. I had taken in the supplies I bought and sat them down in the kitchen. The keys must be in one of the bags. I rummaged through the plastic bags sitting in the floor of the darkened kitchen. It was colder in here because of the caved in corner. I have never been so glad as I was when I found those keys!

In my haste to get up, I slipped and fell back to the floor. Something was emerging from under the house. "Not another damn corpse!" It was a naked girl. She looked me in the eyes, and I knew her at once.

Bibiana Mendez. Always Bibi to me. She and her father had worked briefly for my grandparents. She was fourteen at the time, beautiful, and the first girl I ever kissed.

In death she had remained the same age as when I last saw her, only now her throat was slit from ear to ear. Who could have done such a thing to her?

It suddenly hit me. The looker in the window was her father, Senon Mendez.

Why were their spirits haunting this place above all others? They were alive when they left the farm, or were they?

A voice called out over my shoulder, "Corey," and I knew it was grandpa. *Don't the dead ever die anymore?* "Get over here and leave that spic bitch alone! She got what was coming to her. Last thing I wanted was a half-breed in the family."

He was wearing overalls that were both dirty and bloody. I backed up horrified, "You did this to her?"

"I did this for you. These spics are like rats that have been allowed to overpopulate. It's kinda like deer season…" His logic made me sick.

"How many did you kill?" I couldn't believe I was having this conversation, but not much of the last twenty-four hours could be explained away rationally.

"Not enough, I can tell you that much. Bout' fifteen years worth. Started off dumpin em' out back past the pond. The young ones I took fishin' at the pond." I doubled over and lost what little food I had.

"Can't abide by a weak stomach in this family. I need you strong. There's still a lot of work to do." He couldn't seriously think I was going to help him. I had heard enough. It was time to leave. "Boy, don't you walk away from me when I'm a' talkin' to you!" He was furious.

I had made it over the first hill on the gravel road leading back into town when I noticed my grandpa sitting next to me. I sped up hoping the further I got from the farm the weaker he would get. "I really hate to do this boy, but I guess you're just as bad as she was. Takes two to tango."

He grabbed the wheel and jerked it violently. I fought for control of the wheel, and I realized for the first time that I was doing so because I wanted to live. I wasn't ready to be a corpse yet. I had to tell someone my family's dark secret. Grandpa was strong, and the gravel was loose. The ditches on either side of the country road were deep and thick with forest.

I lost control and left the road. The mustang tumbled and smashed into a tree. I felt the impact throughout my entire being. My soul disconnected upon impact. When I had all my life before me, I lost my will to live. When I had all my life behind me, I found it once again. Now I have neither, but I do have an eternity on earth to think things over. Lucky me.

More than a million people die annually in automobile accidents. Makes you wonder how many truly are accidents. I wonder how Mr. Kline's death got coded? Was he just another traffic fatality or was he classified as a suicide?

From a rural Missouri farmhouse infested with victims and their murderer we move now to the Halloween plight of aspiring actor Justin Case in middle Tennessee.

CHAPTER TWENTY:
HAUNTED EARS:
JUSTIN CASE (SUCH A PRETTY FACE)

I died in the predawn hours of Halloween the year before last. I was returning home to Whites Creek, Tennessee, from the set of *Fools From the Hill*, the movie I had been working on as an extra. The director had been impressed with me and beefed up my role, but still I have very little screen time. It was a start. It was my chance to get discovered. I had always known I was destined to be a star.

It was on Clarksville Highway that I realized my eyelids were getting heavy. I had been sipping from a flask of rum I kept under the seat. It always helped me unwind, but that night it just made me tired. I was battling sleep and would awaken with a spasm of awareness that I had dozed off again. I would right my course, but the cycle would repeat.

Dreams would beckon me to indulge in them and enjoy the warm comfort they offered me in return. A handsome young man was leading me by the hand but to what destination he aspired, I had not a clue. It was a disjointed vision, interrupted by brief spells of alertness time after time. Always I felt his hand holding mine when my eyes close again though. "Justin," I heard the young man call my name as we approached a bright light. The dream ended.

I found my car wrecked at rest in a ditch. My forehead was bleeding, but luckily I found no facial wounds likely to leave a noticeable scar in its wake. My left arm was cut deep, however it would be a small thing to hide a scar there. I tried to back the car out of the ditch. The wheels only spun. It was hard to think clearly. I was tired and disoriented. I sat there in the car with the engine running and reached again for my flask. I downed a few drinks, lidded it, and then let the engine's humming lull me back to sleep. I wasn't ready to deal with this just yet.

I heard footfalls and slamming doors. I observed random images that so often haunt dreams. Two hens and a rooster walked down the road. A little girl sat peering down from a tree losing its blood red leaves to the breeze. She was missing an eye, and the rest of her features where hidden in the darkness and distance between us. I found myself yet wounded and in the company of the mystery teen from my dream. There was another, younger boy with him. We were standing in someone's leaf-covered yard. No lights were on in the house, but the porch swing swayed unevenly in the wind. I heard its chains rattling while I studied the two youths before me.

The younger boy had curly brown hair and gray eyes. He could have been no more than nine years old. He would have looked as picture perfect if he had smiled, but he wore his melancholy like a protective veil, never once raising it.

The older boy looked to be in his middle to late teens. His brown hair was straight, long and suited him well. Ocean-blue was the hue of his eyes. His lips were full and designed for pouting. Both boys stood silent.

"Do you live here?" They just stared at me in reply, so I pointed to the house and asked again, "Is that your house?" Still they did not reply. I cupped my bleeding arm as I spoke. Blood gushed down over my fingers. "It seems I have cut my arm pretty good. Could I trouble you for a towel or something to wrap it in?" My breath reeked of rum.

It was the younger boy that first spoke. "We can't go inside, mister. We've been bad. Dad caught us riding our bikes in the road." He rubbed his eyes, and his older brother – I assumed – pulled him closer.

I knelt down to his level and asked, "What's your name?"

"Mikey."

"Well, Mikey," I replied, "it is late, and I am sure your father is ready to forgive you and your brother." He smiled and told me his brother's name was Brad, and that the girl in the tree was their little sister Anne.

Brad spoke in a much cooler tone, "Don't lie to him! You don't know our father. You don't know what he is like. He isn't the one that makes us stay out here. That is mother's decision."

"Can I speak to your mother? Maybe I can talk to her for you. I have to get this cut cleaned up." The boys laughed. It angered me to be taken lightly.

"I can fix it, mister!" Mikey walked over to me and placed her hands on the cut. His little hands were soon covered in blood. I was puzzled. What could he do to help? I searched for answers in Brad's entrancing eyes. He stood silent returning my stare. I felt Mikey kiss the wound. Repulsed, I pulled away from him and studied my arm. The wound was completely healed; or rather it was as if it had never been injured. *Looks like I won't have to hide that scar either!*

Mikey walked back over to Brad's side. His lips wore my blood, and it was unnerving to behold. As uncomfortable as I was, I owed a debt to this little boy with the ability to heal. "How can I ever repay you?"

He wasted no time replying, "Help Anne down out of the tree. She's stuck." It seemed a simple enough undertaking. I wondered why Brad hadn't already helped her. As I walked through the yard, I noticed blood was indeed covering all the yard's leaves and smearing my shoes more with each step. I vowed to help the little girl down and wake from what had started out as a harmless dream but was slowly sliding into nightmare territory.

Under the tree I felt blood dripping from the remaining leaves. The bark and branches were red and slick and stank like a slaughterhouse. I could see Anne's outline way up in the tree, but as I climbed higher and higher I found I was going to be behind her when I got to her level. She was slender and had not filled out yet. Obviously she was a tomboy.

"Come here, Anne. I'm gonna help you down." She quickly wrapped her arms and legs around me. We began our descent. Halfway down I realized that the girl I was carrying had no face! One eye was resting on her meat-covered skull. I lost all concentration and control. Together, we plummeted to the ground. Instead of finding myself in pain on the ground, I woke up in my car with the engine yet running.

The dream was over. I was safe and sound back in the rational world. No trees bled nor shed leaves drenched in blood. No chickens marched without reason down the road. There were no children around with or without faces.

I felt a sharp pain under my right ear. I had not noticed any cuts there prior to falling asleep. I surveyed it in the mirror. To my horror the little cut I found was steadily getting bigger, and it felt as if something had a hold on me. I guessed I was going into shock when I started seeing a vapor behind me. Then, it began to thicken and become better defined. Soon I could see a hand pulling at the cut, and the mirror showed me my tormentor, Brad. Standing outside the car on either side were Mikey and Anne. Mikey's lips were still as covered in my blood as before. Anne was still faceless and bloody.

The pain was horrible, but I was paralyzed by fear and pain. The children laughed. I gazed through the windshield to find yet another specter watching my torture. A haggard man with torn clothes stood watching me from the other side of the ditch and clutching a bottle of scotch. His expression told me he hated me, but for what I did not know. I had no way of knowing what it all meant. I didn't want to know either. I just sought to free myself. I commanded my limbs to move, and slowly I regained control of my body.

I opened the car door and lunged out, taking my dangling face with me. The air burned my bare facial muscles. One eye was hanging out of the socket. I could still see with the other one when my hair didn't obscure my field of vision. I ran passed Mikey and out into the road. Lights were fast approaching, and they brought with them more pain. I never actually saw the vehicle.

The family was standing over me. Their voices made no sense. Either my ears no longer worked or I was between realms. Anne leaned over me and pulled free my facial flesh. She surrendered it to Brad who lovingly placed it on her.

The driver of the vehicle that hit me called 911, but I was dead long before the ambulance arrived. Do I know now what it all meant? Have I gained understanding? Yes.

Ten years prior to the night in the same place another wreck had occurred. Their alcoholic father had plowed the two boys down while they were riding their bikes in the street. The car had been speeding along so fast that it skidded into the tree where Anne had been climbing. The impact knocked her out of the tree and down on to the car's hood. Her head had been turned completely around and had shattered the windshield. Very little of her face remained. The father died on impact, leaving a dead body that reeked of scotch.

Fools From the Hill was released, but you'll find me nowhere in it. My scenes were cut because I died during production, and another was given my role.

CHAPTER TWENTY-ONE:
RELEASE

As you can probably tell, I wrote at a frantic pace during those days. It was the only way that I could keep my nerves at bay.

I could not sleep the night preceding my release. I lay awake listening to my new cellmate sawing logs after he finished masturbating. These were just a few of the things that I would not miss about prison. Come to think of it, there was nothing I was going to miss about Pollack.

The food sucked. Your neighbors were violent offenders, sexual predators, and liars and thieves. The atmosphere was one of constant violence and fear, which was to be expected in a prison environment. Freedom I did not fear as compared to continuing my years in Pollack.

The guards came for me around seven in the morning. They brought me a box for my belongings. Anything that didn't fit, I left for my new cellie. All I needed was my writings, photos, and letters.

Our first stop was the infirmary so that I could be medically cleared for release. After I was given a full physical, they allowed me to get dressed in street clothes they provided. It was only then, that I truly felt I was indeed going to be a free man once again.

While I waited for them to check for to make sure I had no other warrants or holds on me, I sat romantically dreaming of what it was going to be like to see my first sunrise as a free man in four years. Sure I had seen the sun daily over my prison stint, but from within chain link and razor wire. There would be no towers casting shadows, or guards with rifles waving away the sweat from their brows.

At last our rouse was drawing to its conclusion, as I, the last man out, made my final walk to freedom. I was escorted through many locked checkpoints along with three other inmates whose time had come. When the gate to the outside finally opened, I found Ben patiently waiting, leaning on a limousine.

He was immaculately dressed in a three piece

suit, and looked like he was there as counsel for an inmate. He seemed to have certainly done well for himself.

The driver came around and opened the trunk and stowed my belongings for me. Ben hugged me, and whispered into my ear, "I don't know how you managed to pull this off you crazy son of a bitch, but it's good to have you out of that place."

"It's good to be out too, trust me."

We were driven to a nearby restaurant that served Italian food. It was nearly noon, and I had missed morning chow. I was hungry like no other. As we waited eagerly to be served, I commented on the limousine waiting for us outside, "So you always travel with such fashion?"

"Usually, but I figured this occasion called for it if no other. Don't get used to it though. We aren't riding in that back to Dexter."

"We aren't?" I was disappointed. It was my first time in a limo and found myself thinking that I could really get used to it.

"Nope. We are riding down to the Pineville Municipal Airport where I have chartered us a plane." He said. I was impressed. I was also relieved to be putting fast distance between Pollack and myself.

Our waiter, an androgynous waif with piercing and tattoos, brought out our water and a bottle of pinot.

The meal was splendid, but the wine was better. As we ate, I told Ben how I had come to procure and early release. I also confided in him my plans to retire to Thailand. I asked him to join me and Lenny.

"Well you certainly have the money." He opened

up his brief case and pushed a piece of paper my way. It was a bank statement with a number and many zero's following it. "Interest accrues, and off the top of my head I'd say with the current exchange rates you've got about thirty-two million Baht." He smiled. "I'll think about the offer."

"Ok, so I can afford it. What about you Mr. Benjamin? Have you really done so brilliantly for yourself or is this all smoke and mirrors?" I asked.

He leaned in, smiled, and said, "Son, I make almost as much as you have in that account, daily. I think I can afford it."

When we were finished we returned to the limousine. The driver was ready and waiting with the door open for us.

"I hate to ask since you have already done so much for me, Ben, but I have one more favor to ask you." Ben nodded and waited for me to continue. "There are two more people I would like to invite to Thailand. Could I use your phone?"

"Sure." Phone in hand, I dialed Slick's number.

Nick answered the phone high, which didn't really surprise me. Honestly, I was shocked he had not ended up back in custody.

We talked for about twenty minutes, and I told him my plans. I told him that, eventually what we had done would be discovered, and that we needed to get out of the country while we had the chance.

I told him to say his goodbyes, and we would meet him in New Orleans in two weeks. Katie was invited also. I would be wiring him some money to get their documentation in order and buy some luggage and what not. It didn't take much convincing beyond that.

I handed the phone back to Ben, grabbed a bottle from the mini-bar, downed it, and laid my head back to rest my eyes.

I must have dosed off because we were at the airport before I knew it. I woke up in the limo alone. I rapped on the window, and the driver informed me that Ben had gone to sign and pay for the plane.

Soon Ben returned and instructed the driver to take us to our plane. As we pulled up to the Raytheon Premiere One, I was instantly taken with the aircraft. In the past few hours I had gone from thinking vending machine munchies were a luxury to being chauffeured around in a stretched limousine and was about to board a private jet. I had gone from having not even my freedom to the world being my oyster.

We boarded and received our safety briefing. The cabin was beautifully clad in white leather. It had room for seven, not counting the crew, and though I knew that we were not struggling with money, I wondered why Ben had not opted for a smaller, cheaper plane?

He seemed to read my mind, and answered, "It was the cheapest they had."

I smiled and replied, "Oh, man that sucks." We both laughed and prepared for takeoff. With a cruising speed of just over 450 miles an hour we would be home in about an hour. I was grateful for the haste of the travel accommodations Ben had lined up, but I would not have minded the trip taking a little longer.

It was my first chance to view the world from forty-one thousand miles up, and it filled me with awe. On the ascent I watched the people and automobiles scurry about. I watched the sun's reflection pass across the waterways. The cookie cutter houses arranged in geometric patters or nestled tightly lining the little streets amused me. Our trajectory increased steeply, and we climbed through the clouds, finally flying high above them.

We touched down a little past four at Dexter's small airport. That was another beautiful thing about using a smaller, private jet; there was no need to fly all the way to Saint Louis or Memphis and drive the rest of the way to Dexter.

As we were getting off the jet, I noticed my shadow growing long in the afternoon sun. Even in the darkest night, my shadow would always be with me, waiting for my return into the light, and it would carry my past deeds and regrets as surely as I would always carry both the loving memories and scars they had caused. No matter what I bought or where I went, the only thing that would ever belong to me was my accumulation of mistakes and lessons learned.

I would teach my son, Lenny, the best that I could. I would use my wealth and time to provide him with a more cultured and fulfilling life than either his mother or I had known. If my shadow held my past, it was surely my son that was my bright future.

Twenty minutes later, yet another limousine arrived to fetch us. I would have been fine riding in a taxi, but, once again, Ben insisted. "This will be the first time you have gotten to see your son in four years, AJ. Mrs. Foxworth needs to know that you are capable and ready to be the father we both know you are. Present the image. Image is everything."

Still, I felt strange, riding through Dexter in a limousine, like a rock star or celebrity with no real claim to fame other than the obvious.

We pulled on to West Oak Street, the street the Foxworth's house was on. Everyone notices a limo in a small town like Dexter. Kids playing at the park across the street just stared. The allure of power, money and fame seemed to stop them in their tracks.

I could hear people in the distance starting to talk. "Isn't that…"

"He looks just like AJ Jackson."

"Is that him?"

People were gathering across the street in the gravel parking area buffering the park from the road. I was taken aback by the attention as we walked to the porch and knocked.

"This is what image gets you, Ben," I said. "Too much attention."

CHAPTER TWENTY-TWO:
FINAL DESTINATION

The red door opened. It seemed to take forever to open. I couldn't help but shed a tear at the sight before me. The sweetest word ever uttered rushed me, "Dad?"

Little Lenny was not so little any more. His hair had darkened a little. He kept it cut short. His eyes were still as clear as ever. I could see my Christi in his every move and mannerism.

I smiled that smile that only parents know how to smile. Every parent knows the emotion; being overwhelmed by your child's complete and utter perfection. The love rushes into your soul, filling it up until you think you will simply explode.

I remembered exactly the last time I had felt the emotion. It was eight years prior as I watched Lenny sleep at Ben's house.

Lenny rushed to hug me. Everything in the world was perfect in that moment that seemed to go on forever yet ended too soon.

He stood there smiling that smile that was his mother's through and through. I turned to check on the crowd still gathering across the street and found it growing larger. "Let's go inside, son."

Lenny led the way with Ben and I following him inside. The house, like most every house, had its own distinctive scent, that of its occupants. It was not off-putting, but was still noticeable. There were two small potted ferns hanging from the ceiling, one on each side of the large picture window. What seemed like a thousand books lined the bookshelves.

The flat screen television Lenny had been watching when we arrived was still on, blaring the evening news rather than rap videos. I felt pride rush over me that my boy kept up on current events.

We sat down, and I had Lenny turn the volume down. We needed to talk. I needed to know who he wanted to live with now that I was out. I wanted him to come with me, but I wanted it to be his decision.

"Len, um, I'm moving overseas, and I would like for you to come live with me… if that is what you want," I said. "I know this is all sudden, but it is just the way it has to be, son. If you wanna stay here, with your grandma Foxworth, I'll understand too."

He said nothing. His gaze dropped to the carpet

as he mulled over what I had said. I glanced up to the television, and noticed that the front of the house was being broadcast on the cable news channel.

The ticker-tape scrolling across the bottom of the screen read: JACKSON FREE, RETURNS TO DEXTER, MO.

I peeked through the curtain and saw that three reporters were already posted up outside. The crowd of onlookers was still slowly growing.

I began to realize that this was a bad idea. I was fresh out of prison and already Lenny was being drug into the circus that was my life. But wasn't that why I was here; to escape with him to the outer reaches of my infamy? His voice drew my attention back.

"I love you, dad," he began, "and I always will. Dexter is home. I don't want to move away." My heart sank, and he quickly added, "But I'll come visit as much as you'll let me this summer."

I tried to hide my disappointment. I put on a fake smile, but Ben knew. "Yeah, Len, sure. We'll have a great time. I should be settled in by then."

"Can you stay tonight?" He asked.

"Sure. I was hoping to take you and your grandparents out to eat. Where would you like to go? Anywhere you want, just name it."

"Well, I haven't been to Hickory Log in awhile," he offered. At the very mention of the restaurant's name, my mouth began watering, as I thought about their enticing pork ribs. In all my travels, I have never found any other restaurant with ribs that can compare to those at the Hickory Log, so I was sold on the idea in an instant.

I stayed with the Foxworths' for a few days before I decided it was time to leave and- with my departure- restore peace and quiet to this usually-sleepy little town I had grown up in so long ago. Sure, I had outgrown Dexter, but Lenny had not. His grandparents' home was stable. It was his home base, where nothing could harm him.

He had grown into such a fine young man. What can I say? This father's pride knows no bounds. Before I left, I made sure that he realized just how special he was to me.

Two weeks later I arrived in New Orleans with only an hour before my connecting flight to Thailand by way of Los Angeles, California. Nick and woman were waiting for me. Ben had gone home to get his affairs in order, but planned to join us in a few weeks.

"Bout time, playa!" Slick yelled. We shook hands, and he introduced me to his woman, Katie.

Over the loudspeaker I heard the announcement that boarding for our flight was starting. I glanced over at Slick, "You ready for this?"

"The question is, is Thailand ready for dis? Cheap beer, cheaper women!" He stopped to dodge Katie's incoming slap. "Relax, woman, I'm just playing." As she looked away, he shook his head; a clear signal that Thailand was about to get more than it ever bargained for with AJ Jackson, and Slick and Katie Goode as the newest residents.

I'm not going to tell you I'll never have more to write about my travels. In all likelihood, I will have plenty of adventures to share with you, but I just don't know when I'm gonna feel like pausing the living to do the writing. Since I'm not telling, I guess time will have to do it for me.

THE
END